GOVERNMENT PROCEDURES AND OPERATIONS

EMINENT DOMAIN

USES, EFFECTS, AND CIVIL RIGHTS IMPLICATIONS OF ITS ABUSE

GOVERNMENT PROCEDURES AND OPERATIONS

Additional books in this series can be found on Nova's website under the Series tab.

Additional e-books in this series can be found on Nova's website under the e-book tab.

GOVERNMENT PROCEDURES AND OPERATIONS

EMINENT DOMAIN

USES, EFFECTS, AND CIVIL RIGHTS IMPLICATIONS OF ITS ABUSE

IRENE HINES
EDITOR

nova publishers
New York

NOTICE TO THE READER

Additional color graphics may be available in the e-book version of this book.

Library of Congress Cataloging-in-Publication Data

ISBN: 978-1-63483-440-7

Published by Nova Science Publishers, Inc. † New York

CONTENTS

PREFACE

The Fifth Amendment to the U.S. Constitution states that government shall not take private property except for "public use" and with "just compensation." Officials from national organizations and state and local governments cited various purposes for which eminent domain can be or has been used, including the building or expansion of transportation-related projects; the elimination and prevention of conditions that are detrimental to the physical, social, and economic well-being of an area; remediation of environmental contamination; and economic development. This book provides information on the purposes for and extent to which eminent domain can be and has been used; the process states and select localities across the country use to acquire land, including by eminent domain; how the use of eminent domain has affected individuals and communities in select localities; and the changes state legislatures made to laws governing the use of eminent domain from June 2005 through July 2006.

In: Eminent Domain
Editor: Irene Hines
ISBN: 978-1-63483-440-7

Chapter 1

EMINENT DOMAIN: INFORMATION ABOUT ITS USES AND EFFECT ON PROPERTY OWNERS AND COMMUNITIES IS LIMITED*

United States Government Accountability Office

ABBREVIATIONS

DOT	Department of Transportation
FHWA	Federal Highway Administration
HUD	Department of Housing and Urban Development
STIP	Statewide Transportation Improvement Program
URA	Uniform Relocation Assistance and Real Property Acquisition Policies Act of 1970

WHY GAO DID THIS STUDY

In the Transportation, Treasury, Housing and Urban Development, the Judiciary, the District of Columbia, and Independent Agencies Appropriations Act, 2006, Congress mandated that GAO conduct a nationwide study on the use of eminent domain by state and local governments. This report provides

* This is an edited, reformatted and augmented version of a report, GAO-07-28, issued by the Government Accountability Office, dated November 2006.

information on (1) the purposes for and extent to which eminent domain can be and has been used; (2) the process states and select localities across the country use to acquire land, including by eminent domain; (3) how the use of eminent domain has affected individuals and communities in select localities; and (4) the changes state legislatures made to laws governing the use of eminent domain from June 2005 through July 2006.

To address these objectives, GAO reviewed relevant provisions in federal, state, and local laws; conducted site visits to various redevelopment projects where eminent domain was used; and interviewed multiple national associations of local and state government officials and planning professionals, national public interest groups, and national property rights groups to gain their perspectives on the use of eminent domain and its effect on communities and property owners.

WHAT GAO FOUND

Officials from national organizations and state and local governments cited various purposes for which eminent domain can be or has been used, including the building or expansion of transportation-related projects; the elimination and prevention of conditions that are detrimental to the physical, social, and economic well-being of an area; remediation of environmental contamination; and economic development. However, no centralized or aggregate national or state data exist on the use of eminent domain, thereby precluding GAO from any national or statewide assessments of, among other things, how frequently eminent domain is used for private-to-public or private-to-private transfer of property and purposes of these transfers.

Multiple laws promulgated from federal, state, and local governments set forth how authorities can acquire land—including by eminent domain— and how compensation for property owners is determined. Some believe payment limits are too low. The initial step in a project that involves land acquisition is the public review and approval by a public body of a project plan, which is followed by a land valuation process during which title studies and appraisals are completed. During the land acquisition stage, authorities often make a formal offer to the owner and attempt to negotiate the purchase of the property. If the authority cannot locate the owner or the parties cannot agree to a price, among other circumstances, the authorities then begin the formal legal proceedings to acquire the property by eminent domain. Finally, once the property is acquired, authorities may provide relocation assistance that may include monetary payments to cover moving expenses.

Redevelopment projects for which eminent domain is used affect individuals and communities in a range of ways that cannot be quantified due to a lack of measures and aggregate data. According to authorities, areas selected for redevelopment could have been vacant and abandoned land or those that included residents and operating businesses. Local officials both described and showed us community benefits resulting from redevelopment projects, including additional employment opportunities and housing in an area. Also, property rights groups told us some of the negative effects of eminent domain, such as the dispersal of long-standing communities. Finally, these groups expressed concerns about how authorities implement procedures for using eminent domain, particularly the provision of public notice to owners about the risk of condemnation, and the process for designating an area as blighted.

From June 23, 2005, through July 31, 2006, 29 states enacted at least one of the following three general types of changes to their eminent domain laws:

1. restrictions on the use of eminent domain under certain circumstances,
2. additional procedural requirements, and (3) changes that defined or redefined key terms related to eminent domain including public use.

* * *

November 30, 2006

The Honorable Christopher S. Bond
Chairman

The Honorable Patty Murray
Ranking Member
Subcommittee on Transportation,
Treasury, the Judiciary, Housing and Urban
Development, and Related Agencies
Committee on Appropriations
United States Senate

The Honorable Joe Knollenberg
Chairman

The Honorable John W. Olver
Ranking Member
Subcommittee on Transportation,
Treasury, Housing and Urban Development,
The Judiciary, District of Columbia, and
Independent Agencies
Committee on Appropriations
House of Representatives

The protection of property rights plays a vital role within a market economy by allowing property owners to control their property and therefore benefit from its use, sale, or value. However, elected federal, state, and local government officials long have relied on eminent domain— the government's power to take private property for a public use while fairly compensating the property owner—to assemble land needed to meet their constituents' various public needs. The debate surrounding the use of eminent domain by state and local governments was invigorated by the 2005 United States Supreme Court decision in *Kelo v. City of New London* (*Kelo* decision), which involved the purpose for which a government authority can invoke its eminent domain power.[1] The decision allows private-to-private transfer of property for economic revitalization purposes pursuant to a city development plan.

In the Transportation, Treasury, Housing and Urban Development, the Judiciary, the District of Columbia, and Independent Agencies Appropriations Act, 2006 (2006 Act), Congress included provisions addressing the use of eminent domain for private-to-private transfers of property for economic development purposes.[2] The 2006 Act also mandated that we conduct a nationwide study on the use of eminent domain. Focused on state and local government use of eminent domain, this report provides information on (1) the purposes for and extent to which eminent domain can be and has been used; (2) the process states and select localities across the country use to acquire land, including by eminent domain; (3) how the use of eminent domain has affected individuals and communities in select localities; and (4) the changes state legislatures made to laws governing the use of eminent domain from June 2005 through July 2006.

To address these objectives, we reviewed constitutional provisions in all 50 states to determine whether states require a public use in order to invoke eminent domain and that "just" compensation (generally fair market value) be paid to property owners whose property is acquired through eminent domain. We conducted site visits to five cities— Baltimore, Chicago, Denver, Los

Angeles, and New York—where we toured projects for which eminent domain was used; reviewed detailed project-specific documentation, and interviewed local officials, property rights groups, and property owners to document their respective positions and concerns about eminent domain use within their communities. In addition, we interviewed multiple national associations of local and state government officials and planning professionals, national public interest groups, and national property rights groups to gain their perspectives on the use of eminent domain and its effect on communities and property owners. From some of these national organizations, we solicited project examples in which eminent domain was used. We interviewed officials from 10 state-level departments of transportation on their land acquisition practices, including the use of eminent domain. Furthermore, we interviewed officials at the U.S. Departments of Transportation, Housing and Urban Development, and Justice, and the Environmental Protection Agency about how federal programs or funding may be involved in eminent domain proceedings undertaken by state and local governments. Finally, we monitored changes to provisions of eminent domain laws from June 2005 through July 2006 in 50 states. In addressing our objectives, the lack of comprehensive data on the use of eminent domain in states across the nation limited the scope of our work and our methodological options.

We conducted our work from January through November 2006 in accordance with generally accepted government auditing standards. Appendix I discusses our scope and methodology in further detail.

RESULTS IN BRIEF

Officials from national organizations, states, and cities with whom we spoke cited common public purposes for which eminent domain can be or has been used, but limited data preclude a determination of the extent to which eminent domain has been used nationwide. Purposes cited included building roads and other transportation-related projects, construction of state and municipal facilities, the elimination and prevention of blight, remediation of environmental contamination, and economic development.[3] We obtained data on the specific instances and purposes for which eminent domain had been used from selected state departments of transportation and local authorities. For example, officials from state departments of transportation that we contacted reported collecting some information related to their use of eminent domain, such as the number of properties or portions of properties acquired through eminent domain. According to information provided by Baltimore city officials, their city most often invoked its eminent domain power to assemble land for redevelopment projects that involved blight removal, while Los Angeles officials said that the city most often used it for street improvements. Although some selected state departments of transportation and local authorities provided us data on their eminent domain use, no aggregate national or state data exist, thereby precluding us from any statewide or national assessments of (1) how frequently eminent domain is used, (2) how often private-to-public or private-to-private transfer of property occurs, or (3) the purposes for which eminent domain has been used by state and local governments. The data limitations result from factors such as multiple authorities within a state having power to invoke eminent domain and states not having central depositories to collect such data. For example, in Virginia, no state agency tracks the use of eminent domain by the at least 40 types of authorities (such as school boards) that have the power.

Although federal, state, and local laws and regulations direct how property owners will be compensated when eminent domain is used, the basic procedural requirements for invoking eminent domain exhibit similarities nationwide. Federal and state constitutions and laws outline how property owners whose land is being acquired through eminent domain should be compensated. In addition, federal and state laws establish relocation benefits for displaced residents and businesses. In particular, when authorities acquire property for a project in which federal funds are involved, states and localities become subject to the Uniform Relocation Assistance and Real Property Acquisition Policies Act of 1970 (URA), which establishes relocation payment amounts and procedures.[4] However, many state and local officials commented that the limits the URA places on certain relocation expenditures were too low and needed to be revised. State and local laws also set forth basic procedural requirements—which share certain similarities nationwide—for how authorities acquire land, including by eminent domain.[5] These procedures can be divided broadly into four stages or steps. The initial step is project planning, during which a public body can consider and approve a redevelopment plan, which outlines the need for the project and identifies parcels required to complete the project. After such plans are approved, authorities typically begin the land valuation process, during which they conduct title studies to determine legal ownership of needed parcels and complete appraisals. During the third stage, land acquisition, authorities often make a formal offer to an owner and attempt to negotiate the purchase of the property. If the authority and the property owner cannot agree to a price or if an authority cannot locate an owner, the authority then begins the formal legal proceedings to acquire the property by eminent domain. Finally, once the property has been acquired, either through negotiated purchase or eminent domain, authorities must compensate the owner justly and provide relocation assistance that can include payments for moving and related expenses.

The projects in which eminent domain is used generate benefits and costs that affect, whether positively or negatively, a wide range of community interest and individuals. Furthermore, it is difficult to establish measures to quantify the wide range of costs and benefits to individual communities of projects involving eminent domain. In addition, aggregate data on eminent domain use and frequency, as well as costs and benefits, are not available, which would be necessary to examine the impact of eminent domain on a community. Based on the projects that we reviewed or visited, we noted that the areas slated for redevelopment exhibited a variety of conditions. For example, some areas contained vacant and unutilized land and structures and some contained operating businesses and occupied residences. For selected projects where eminent domain was used that we reviewed or visited, authorities described the previously existing conditions of the areas and they told us or we observed some of the benefits realized by communities after the projects were completed. Local officials and officials from most of the selected projects told us that the areas generally could be characterized by different conditions, such as modernized roadways, additional housing, and increased commercial activity. Meanwhile, property rights groups we interviewed described some of the negative effects of eminent domain use, such as assembled land going unused. Property rights groups and a national community organization also highlighted other negative effects, such as loss of small businesses and jobs, decreases in affordable housing, and the dispersal of communities. In addition to these losses, the groups also noted that the ways in which authorities implement procedures for using eminent domain also could adversely affect property owners. They cited examples such as lack of notice, blight designations that negatively impacted neighboring nonblighted properties, significantly undervalued appraisals, and inadequate compensation.

From June 23, 2005, through July 31, 2006, many states enacted changes to their eminent domain laws. According to our analysis, 29 states enacted at least one of three general types of changes to their eminent domain laws. First, 23 of the 29 states placed restrictions on the use of eminent domain, such as prohibiting its use to increase property tax revenues, transfer condemned property to a private entity, or assemble land for projects that are solely for economic development. Second, 24 of the 29 states established additional procedural requirements, such as providing further public notice prior to condemnation. Finally, 21 of the 29 states enacted changes that defined or redefined blight or blighted property, public use, or economic development. For example, some states established that economic development and the public benefits resulting from it, including increased tax revenue and increased employment, do not constitute a public use. The remaining 21 states had not enacted changes to their eminent domain laws during that time period based on our analysis. Some state legislatures approved constitutional amendments restricting current eminent domain laws, which were placed on the ballot for voter consideration. In three states, citizen-initiated proposals to amend the state constitution obtained the requisite number of signatures to be placed on a ballot. Finally, some states, including those that did and did not enact any changes, and state associations commissioned studies to determine if any changes were needed to their eminent domain laws.

We provided a draft of this report to the Departments of Justice, Transportation and Housing and Urban Development for their review. The Department of Transportation provided technical comments, which have been incorporated where appropriate. The Departments of Justice and Housing and Urban Development did not have any comment.

BACKGROUND

An inherent right of sovereignty, eminent domain is a government's power to take private property for a public use while compensating the property owner.[6] Eminent domain is also referred to as "appropriation," "condemnation," and "taking." The Fifth Amendment of the United States Constitution expressly restricts the federal government's use of eminent domain; it requires that eminent domain be invoked only for a "public use" and "just compensation" be paid to those whose property has been taken. The Fourteenth Amendment extends the legal requirements of public use *and just compensation to the states through its Due Process Clause. In* addition, states have a number of constitutional provisions, statutes, and case law outlining the various permissible uses of eminent domain, recourse available to property owners, and procedures required to take or evaluate a property. State legislatures generally determine who may use eminent domain by delegating eminent domain authority to state or quasi-public entities, such as housing, transport, and urban renewal authorities, which may exercise that power only for the purpose for which it was established. States may also grant eminent domain authority to local governments, which may further delegate this authority to a designee, such as a development authority or community group. Finally, some states authorize private companies to exercise eminent domain—for example, for the provision of utility services.

Courts have addressed the meaning and application of public use in numerous cases throughout the years. In 2005, the United States Supreme Court, in *Kelo v. City of New London*, upheld the City of New London's authority to use eminent domain to condemn and acquire property located within an area designated as a "distressed municipality," even though the condemned property was not blighted or otherwise in poor condition.[7]This decision allowed for private-to-private transfers of property for economic development purposes, such as New London's action in an area that had experienced decades of economic decline. According to some scholars, the use of eminent domain for such a purpose has been permitted since the "mill acts" of the colonial and pre-Revolutionary period that permitted the flooding of private property to allow the operation of mills downstream; mills were considered the main source of power and closely linked to economic development.[8] The Supreme Court emphasized that the *Kelo* decision did not preclude states from placing further restrictions on the exercise of eminent domain. Many states have been reviewing the use of eminent domain and considering legislative changes or constitutional amendments to control its use.

In addition to the Constitution, the Uniform Relocation Assistance and Real Property Acquisition Policies Act of 1970 sets the federal standard for acquisition of real property for public projects involving federal financial assistance, including prescribing specific benefits, treatment, and protections for those whose property is acquired.[9] The act also contains requirements for property owner notification and property valuation, as well as prohibitions against offers to property owners being less than an approved appraisal value. In addition, the act addresses compensation and seeks to ensure the fair and equitable treatment and protection from disproportionate injury of persons displaced from their homes, businesses, or farms in all projects involving federal financial assistance. The act requires that certain relocation funding be provided when a resident's property is acquired, such as reasonable out-of-pocket moving expenses and relocation advisory services. The relocation funding also includes payments to cover rent increases or downpayments on home purchases in order to assist tenants and owners in relocating to comparable housing, which, at a minimum, is decent, safe, and sanitary.

A number of federal government agencies have acquisition programs where the federal government acquires title to the land through proceedings in federal courts. However, this report focuses on land acquisitions by state or local governments, or their designees.[10]

STATES AND LOCALITIES USED EMINENT DOMAIN FOR VARIOUS PURPOSES AND TO VARYING DEGREES, BUT THE EXTENT OF EMINENT DOMAIN USE IS UNKNOWN DUE TO LIMITED DATA

Officials from national organizations, states, and cities with whom we spoke cited various common public purposes for which eminent domain can be or has been used, but the lack of data precludes a determination of the extent to which eminent domain has been used across the nation. Purposes for which we received examples include the building or expansion of roads and other transportation-related projects; construction of state and municipal facilities; and the elimination and prevention of blight. In addition, officials from some of the national organizations we contacted, which represent state and local governments, property rights groups, urban planning, and home builders, also cited remediation of environmental contamination and economic development. Although we were able to identify some purposes for which eminent domain can be and has been used by certain authorities, we were unable to determine the number of times and the purposes for which eminent domain has been used across the nation because of a lack of centralized or aggregate data.

National Organizations, State Agencies, and City Officials Cited Various Purposes for Using Eminent Domain

According to representatives from some national organizations representing state and local governments, property rights groups, farmers, and planning professionals, and state departments of transportation (DOT) and city officials, eminent domain could be and has been used for various purposes. In particular, many of these representatives and officials said that eminent domain was sometimes needed for the completion of transportation-related projects, such as the building or expansion of roads and highways. As an example, according to Texas DOT officials, from November 1996 through March 2005, the department invoked eminent domain to acquire 6 of the 26 properties needed to assemble land for the construction of an interchange that connected two major highways in central Texas. These officials explained that most of these acquisitions involved the taking of a small portion of the property (partial takings). Furthermore, Texas DOT officials said that because they were making improvements to existing highway facilities, the location of such improvements was limited to properties adjacent to the highway.

In addition, Florida DOT officials told us that the department used eminent domain in 1998 and 1999 to acquire 23 of 51 properties, most of which were partial takings, needed to reconstruct and widen an existing roadway from two to four lanes. City officials we contacted also provided examples of transportation-related projects in which eminent domain was used. For example, an official from a city in Texas told us that the city, in collaboration with the city's transit authority, used eminent domain to acquire 2 of the 9 commercial properties needed to assemble land for the expansion of the city's light rail system in October 1998. According to this official, the city's transit authority was seeking to extend its existing light rail system to provide a low-cost and energy-efficient means of mass transit for commuters.

Another purpose for which eminent domain can be or has been used is the construction or maintenance of state and municipal infrastructure, such as state and municipal buildings. For example, in January 2002, Los Angeles used eminent domain to acquire 2 of the 7 properties needed to assemble land for the construction of a public building that eventually accommodated state and city departments of transportation. In addition, officials from some of the national organizations we contacted said that eminent domain is also used for public utilities. For example, New York City used eminent domain to assemble land for the construction of a tunnel for the city's water system. To complete one phase of the project, the city used eminent domain to acquire 3 of the 10 properties needed to construct support facilities for the operation and maintenance of the water tunnel. Furthermore, the city condemned subsurface rights on more than 1,100 properties for the construction of the Manhattan portion of the tunnel and approximately 640 additional subsurface rights for the Brooklyn and Queens portions. According to a New York City Department of Environmental Protection report, the tunnel is expected to enhance and improve the city's water system and allow for inspection and repair of the city's existing tunnels.[11] In addition, an official from a county in California provided information about the condemnation of 40 parcels of property in June 2001 to assemble land for a flood control and protection project, most of which were partial takings. According to this official, the flood control and protection improvements were intended for public safety and public infrastructure protection.

Eminent domain also can be and has been used to eliminate or prevent blight. For example, according to an official from a community redevelopment agency in Florida, the agency used eminent domain in March 1998 to acquire 3 of the 39 parcels needed to eliminate slum and blighted conditions, stimulate private investment in the area, provide commercial opportunities, and enhance the area's tax base. This agency official said that the redevelopment of the area consists of commercial space and residential housing and was the first significant private investment made in the area in decades. In addition, New York City officials provided an example in which the city condemned property through eminent domain to eliminate blight. According to city officials, the city acquired 407 parcels to eliminate blight by constructing a major housing development.[12] The city's plan for the project indicated that the project was intended to accomplish several things, including providing new and rehabilitated housing for low-, moderate-, and middle-income residents and strengthening the tax base of the city by encouraging development.

Furthermore, officials of some national organizations representing state and local governments, property rights groups, planners, and home builders said that eminent domain can be used for brownfield remediation, which is the environmental cleanup of property that is or may be contaminated. According to officials from an organization representing local government environmental professionals, oftentimes development of certain brownfield properties only occurs with the use of eminent domain because of the owners' unwillingness to transfer property or allow access for site inspections for fear of later being held liable for clean-up costs. Although the officials from the national organizations mentioned above also cited brownfield remediation as a purpose for which eminent domain could be used, we were unable to obtain sufficient project information to conduct any further analysis or provide examples in this report.

Finally, officials from some of the national organizations with whom we met cited economic development as a purpose for which eminent domain can be and has been used. However, according to an official from a national organization representing city governments, the use of eminent domain solely for economic development purposes is minimal compared with the use of eminent domain for other purposes, such as transportation-related projects. Officials from some authorities that have the power to use eminent domain said that some of their projects might be linked to economic development, but that economic development was not the primary purpose of the projects. In addition, all of the projects we reviewed in which eminent domain was used to eliminate blight were associated with projects intended to improve the economic condition of the area. For example, as we have previously described, the redevelopment agency in Florida used eminent domain to acquire three parcels of property to eliminate slum and blighted conditions by stimulating private investment in the area, providing commercial opportunities, and enhancing the area's tax base.

Officials from an organization representing state legislatures said that economic development is closely related to blight removal because authorities with eminent domain power may claim that blight removal will stimulate the community's economic conditions. In addition, representatives from some national organizations representing state and local governments, planning professionals, and officials from some cities we visited said that transportation-related projects might lead to an area's economic development. For example, New York City officials said that even acquisitions of property by eminent domain that are not primarily intended for economic development, such as the construction of a road or highway, would likely improve the economic condition in the area because of the improved access to businesses in the area, potentially increasing the profitability of the businesses. City officials from Chicago and Los Angeles told us that the construction of state buildings in their downtowns had positive economic impact on their cities because the projects attracted private development. Finally, an official from Denver Urban Renewal Authority described the Authority's use of eminent domain to assist a developer complete refurbishing of a downtown property of architectural and historical significance, thus preventing the property from becoming vacant and potentially having a negative impact on its surrounding area.

We also obtained data on the use of eminent domain from selected state DOTs and local authorities.[13] The data reflect that the amount of eminent domain activity and purposes for which eminent domain was invoked *varied by states and localities. Officials from 9 state DOTs we contacted* estimated that the number of individual properties they used eminent domain to acquire in the last 5 years for transportation-related projects ranged from approximately 200 to 7,800.[14] As we previously discussed, according to the state DOT officials, because most of their projects involve improvements on existing transportation systems, the majority of the private properties they assembled for the projects consisted of partial acquisitions.[15] In addition, according to information provided by Baltimore and Los Angeles city officials, Baltimore invoked its eminent domain power most commonly to assemble land for urban redevelopment projects that involved blight removal, while Los Angeles invoked its eminent domain power most often for street improvements projects. Similarly, according to New York City officials, the city invoked its eminent domain power most commonly to assemble land for parks and street widening. Officials from Chicago and Denver told us that they do not have complete data on the number and purposes for which they used their eminent domain authority, but provided us with some information on their use of eminent domain. Specifically, City of Chicago officials estimated that they acquired 2,000 parcels through eminent domain in the last 10 years. In addition, officials from Denver told us that the city used its eminent domain authority mostly for street improvement projects.

No Aggregate Data Exist on the Number of Instances and Purposes for which Eminent Domain Was Used

The lack of state or national data precluded objective statewide or national assessments on the use of eminent domain, including (1) how frequently eminent domain is used, (2) how often private-to-public or private-to-private transfer of property occurs, or (3) the purposes for which eminent domain has been used by state and local governments.[16]Although we were able to collect limited data on the purposes and number of instances in which eminent domain was used, officials from some of the national organizations we contacted told us that state or national aggregate data on the use of eminent domain do not exist. At least two major factors account for the lack of aggregate data. First, officials from the U.S. Departments of Transportation and Housing and Urban Development, as well as the Environmental Protection Agency, told us that the federal agencies generally do not acquire private property through eminent domain directly, but may be indirectly involved through the different programs or agencies they administer or fund. Furthermore, officials from these Federal agencies told us that they do not formally track whether program participants use eminent domain.

Second, the lack of state data on the use of eminent domain may result from multiple authorities in a state having the power to invoke eminent domain and states not having central repositories to collect such data. As we have previously discussed, since states grant eminent domain authorities to local governments, which may further delegate this authority to a designee, such as a development authority, many entities have the power to invoke eminent domain. Of the 10 state legislative research offices we contacted, 5 provided us with information on the authorities that have eminent domain power within their states.[17] For instance, according to information provided by the Virginia legislative research office, at least 40 different types of authorities can invoke eminent domain, including school board districts that can use it to acquire any property necessary for public school purposes. The legislative research office of Massachusetts listed 8 different types of authorities with eminent domain power. For example, the Armory Commission can use eminent domain to acquire land suitable for target practice ranges for the armed forces of Massachusetts, subject to the governor's approval.[18] In addition to the 8 authorities, the information provided by the Massachusetts legislative research office states that Massachusetts' general statutes also grant the power to, among others, the governor and state council, county commissioners, and city aldermen. Furthermore, according to a Texas Legislative Council report, at least 90 different types of authorities have been granted the power of eminent domain in Texas, including agricultural development districts, railroad companies, and sports facilities districts.[19] Finally, the legislative research offices of Illinois and Washington provided us with information on statutes that described the authorities that were granted eminent domain power. In particular, in Illinois, at least 168 types of authorities, including those dealing with transportation, such as the Chicago Transit Authority and the Kankakee River Valley Area Airport Authority, have the power to acquire property through eminent domain, and, in Washington, at least 78 types of authorities were granted this power.

ALTHOUGH MANY LAWS GOVERN LAND ACQUISITION, INCLUDING EMINENT DOMAIN USE, COMMON PRACTICES EXIST NATIONWIDE

Public authorities at the state and local levels acquire property, including by eminent domain, through processes set forth in various federal, state, and local land acquisition laws and implementing regulations. Federal and state laws, such as the URA, outline how much compensation authorities need to pay property owners whose land is being acquired and also direct authorities on what type of relocation assistance to provide to residents and businesses. However, local and state officials we met expressed some concerns about certain limits that the URA places on the amount and type of relocation payments to displaced residents and businesses. In addition to local laws and regulations, federal and state laws establish procedures for how authorities must undertake land acquisition, including the use of eminent domain. Although multiple laws address land acquisition, authorities we interviewed follow broadly similar steps. When acquiring land, which may involve the use of eminent domain, authorities generally follow a four-step process: (1) project planning; (2) property valuation; (3) property acquisition; and (4) relocation of displaced property owners, residents, and businesses. Sometimes these steps overlap.

Federal and State Governments Set Compensation and Relocation Benefits, but Concerns Exist That Some Payment Limits Are Too Low

Land acquisition laws generally require compensation be paid to the owner of a property that a public authority has acquired, including acquisitions by eminent domain. All 50 state constitutions require that just or fair compensation be paid to those whose property has been taken through eminent domain.[20] Just compensation is a payment by the government for property it has taken under eminent domain, usually the fair market value, so that the owner theoretically is no worse off after the taking.[21] As mentioned earlier, the United States Constitution stipulates that eminent domain use by a government authority must include just compensation to the property owner. Some state constitutions, including Georgia and Montana, provide for payment of expenses above the fair market value of the property such as, in certain circumstances, attorney's fees or litigation expenses incurred in determining adequate compensation.

The land acquisition process often includes relocation of either the property owner or residents and businesses located in the property acquired by the authority; federal and state laws also address the costs involved in relocation. Requirements in the URA, the federal law governing the provision of relocation benefits to displaced parties, are applicable to all acquisitions—including voluntary acquisitions achieved through negotiated settlements and acquisitions through eminent domain—of real property for federal or federally assisted programs or projects. The URA provides benefits to displaced individuals, families, businesses, and nonprofit organizations. The types of benefits provided depend on factors such as ownership, tenancy, and use of property (commercial versus residential use). Local officials told us that they have provided benefits under the URA such as: actual moving costs for residents and businesses; comparable replacement housing; rental assistance for tenants; cost of personal property loss for businesses; expenses in finding a replacement site for businesses; and reestablishment costs for businesses up to $10,000.[22] In addition, some city and state officials with whom we spoke explained that their states have adopted legislation or policies with requirements similar to the URA, providing some or all of the same benefits to residents and owners displaced through nonfederally funded projects.[23]

However, local officials, and redevelopment agency officials from four of the five cities we visited believed that payment amounts allowable under the URA might not be adequate to cover costs. For example, we were told that a $10,000 cap on reestablishment costs for business relocation, unchanged since 1987, was too low.[24] Most officials noted that reestablishments costs exceed this cap. For example, Chicago officials described high reestablishment costs such as, replacing specialized fixtures, licensing and permitting, and differential payments for increased rent, insurance, and other needs. Furthermore, a Los Angeles city official noted that the URA requires lump sum payments to remain under a $20,000 cap.[25] Los Angeles officials use these settlements frequently, but one official stated that the URA cap was too low.

Officials from 6 of the 10 state DOTs that we contacted remarked that various benefit limits in the URA are too low to properly compensate for business reestablishment costs. According to the U.S. Department of Transportation, the agency responsible for issuing regulations to implement the URA, the agency's Federal Highway Administration (FHWA) has received comments about the inadequacy of business reestablishment payments under the URA from states, other federal agencies, and affected businesses.[26] In response to these comments, FHWA undertook multiple activities to identify needed programmatic change in the URA, according to FHWA officials. In particular, in 2002 FHWA conducted a study to assess the adequacy of current URA provisions for business relocations and found that reestablishment payments were largely considered inadequate.[27] In 2005 FHWA made some revisions to the URA regulations, but the revisions did not raise the cap on reestablishment payments.[28] Such an increase requires a statutory change.[29]

State and Local Laws Further Direct Authorities on How to Acquire Land, Including Eminent Domain Use

State and local laws further condition how land may be acquired, including through eminent domain (see fig. 1). Among the states that we reviewed, some states enacted additional laws concerning land acquisition, such as requirements for environmental assessments. For instance, according to City of Los Angeles officials, the California Environmental Quality Act requires that the environmental impacts of discretionary projects proposed to be carried out by public agencies, including in general publicly funded projects in the state involving land acquisition, be assessed at the earliest possible time in the environmental review process.[30] In New York, according to city officials, when a significant adverse environmental impact is likely to result from a project, the State Environmental Quality Review Act requires an assessment in the form of an environmental impact statement of short and long term impacts, adverse environmental impacts, and mitigation measures.[31] In addition, according to officials, residential and business displacement from a project is generally analyzed in the review conducted under New York State and New York City law.

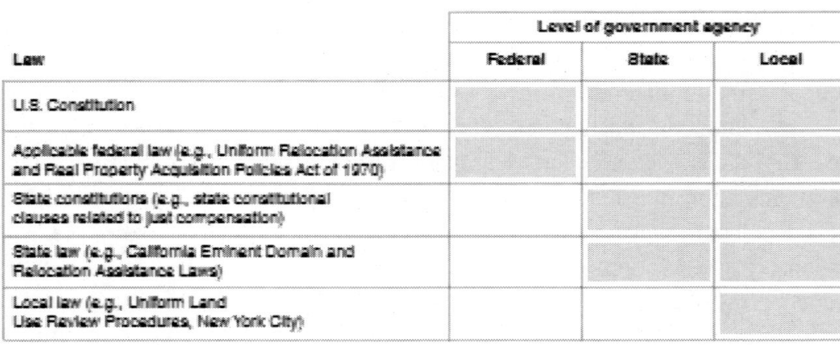

Source: GAO.

Figure 1. Federal, State, and Local Laws Condition the Use of Eminent Domain.

Some states have laws outlining how authorities granted eminent domain authority within their state can invoke this power to assemble land for public projects. For example, in Illinois, Article VII of the Code of Civil Procedure sets forth procedures for use of the power of eminent domain by state and local governments including provisions regarding the determination of property value, negotiation with property owners, and the initiation of condemnation.[32]

Provisions in the Illinois Municipal Code authorize municipalities to take property for redevelopment based on a blight designation.[33] In New York, the Eminent Domain Procedure Law sets forth the procedure by which property is acquired and property owners are compensated.[34] This law also establishes the opportunity for public participation in the planning of redevelopment projects, which may necessitate eminent domain use. Through these procedures, the state acknowledges that the need for public land acquisition should be balanced against the rights of private property owners and local communities, encourages the settlement of claims for compensation, and reduces related litigation. California's Eminent Domain and Relocation Assistance Laws implemented by the Relocation Assistance and Real Property Acquisition Guidelines governs private property acquisition by a public authority not involving federal funds.[35] The guidelines are designed to ensure equitable treatment for persons displaced from a home or business, reduce related litigation, and require comparable replacement dwellings.[36]The Colorado Urban Renewal and Eminent Domain Laws contain procedures for using eminent domain to eliminate or prevent blight or slum conditions.[37] To govern the relocation of displaced residents, Maryland, New York, and Washington, like California, have established laws that provide certain state relocation benefits.[38] Therefore, a mixture of federal and state laws directs how local authorities use their eminent domain power, provide compensation, and other required benefits.

In addition to the federal and state laws that authorities must follow when invoking eminent domain, some of the cities that we visited had additional local laws or city agency regulations that governed urban redevelopment, as well as relocation of displaced residents and businesses (see fig. 1). For example, in New York City, the Uniform Land Use Review Procedure Charter, approved in 1975, standardizes how applications affecting land use in New York City, including projects involving eminent domain, are publicly reviewed.[39] Another law sets forth the rights of residential and commercial tenants displaced by urban redevelopment in New York City.[40]The Los Angeles redevelopment agency has also established an appeals procedure for relocation decisions which is supplementary to federal and state law, according to information provided by Los Angeles city officials.

Authorities Follow Several Similar Steps in Projects that Can Involve Eminent Domain

The complexities associated with land assembly have led to numerous approaches for acquiring land and providing just compensation. However, when state and local authorities acquire land, either through negotiated purchase or eminent domain, they follow some common procedural practices. The land acquisition process generally occurs in four stages, including (1) project planning; (2) property valuation, during which appraisals are conducted; (3) property acquisition; and (4) relocation, during which authorities may provide residents and businesses replacement housing or commercial property (see fig. 2). Sometimes these stages are concurrent, with some variation across the localities we visited. The views that property owners and property rights organizations we interviewed have on these stages are discussed in a later section of this report.

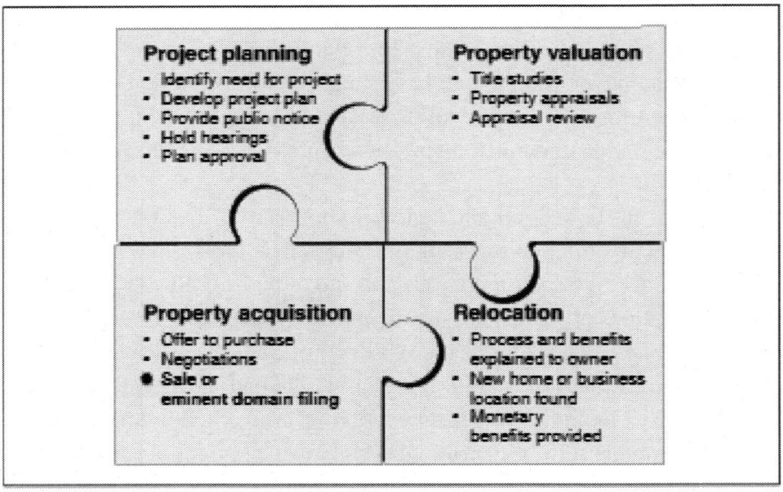

Sources: GAO (analysis); Art Explosion (images).

Figure 2. Common Real Estate Acquisition Stages in Visited Localities.

Project Planning Stage

The project planning stage may begin by identifying the need for a project. Depending on the type of project, city departments of engineering or planning, city redevelopment or renewal authorities, or state departments of transportation with whom we spoke, conduct work at this stage. For example,

23 U.S.C. § 135 (section 135), as amended by the Safe, Accountable, Flexible, Efficient Transportation Equity Act: A Legacy for Users, mandates that states carry out a statewide transportation planning process that involves both a long-range statewide transportation plan, which identifies transportation needs over roughly a 20-year horizon, and a Statewide Transportation Improvement Program (STIP), which is a listing of potential projects to be constructed in the near term, covering a 4-year period.[41]

FHWA and the Federal Transit Administration jointly administer the statewide planning program. During these planning processes, according to FHWA officials, state DOTs work with other state agencies and local authorities within a cooperative, continuous, and comprehensive framework to make decisions on the need for new state highways or interchanges, among other transportation-related public improvements. Section 135 requires public notice during the planning process, which for the long-term plan includes public meetings at convenient and accessible locations at convenient times, use of visualization techniques to describe plans, and provision of public information in an electronically accessible format, such as the Internet.[42] The STIP also requires states to provide interested parties with a reasonable opportunity to comment on the proposed program.[43] According to state DOT officials in New York, project managers will attend local board or council meetings before a design for a new transportation project is proposed. After the project proposal, New York officials hold informational meetings for property owners and allow time for individual question and answer sessions. New York officials consider alternative site selections proposed by the property owners, although the state DOT eventually selects the least intrusive and safest alternative by weighing social, economic, safety, and technical considerations. Other states that we contacted, including Missouri, Illinois, California, Colorado, and Texas, also described their adherence to the federal requirements in conducting their statewide transportation improvement plans and providing public notice of the project design process.

In cities or localities, the project planning stage may generally involve developing, publicly vetting, and approving a project plan by a public body, such as a city council. Redevelopment where eminent domain may be used in the five cities we visited may involve the creation and approval of an urban renewal or redevelopment plan, which establishes such things as the need for the project, lists the parcels required to complete the project, and creates a timeline. In some localities, such planning processes may involve the completion of impact studies of the potential effects from the proposed redevelopment project on the neighborhood and the environment. Multiple public hearings or meetings may occur when localities are vetting a redevelopment plan. Chicago officials told us that the public may attend hearings or meetings held by the city's planning department, city council, and an appointed body known as the Community Development Commission, at which redevelopment plans and takings are approved. In addition, local alderman may also sponsor public meetings on proposed redevelopment plans. In New York City, the Uniform Land Use Procedure Law provides for review before four city entities: the local community board, borough president, city planning commission, and the city council. Property owners and the community, in New York, Chicago and in other localities, are notified about hearings through letters sent to their mailing addresses.

This planning process often ends with the approval of a project plan by a public body. In all five cities we visited, officials told us that the city council approves the redevelopment or urban renewal plan, at times granting the appropriate public authority the specific power to acquire properties necessary to complete the project. Sometimes the development of these plans involves organizations outside the local or state government, such as community groups or developers. Officials from some of the cities we visited explained that the city may work with the developer by exercising its power of eminent domain to complete the site assemblage necessary for a developer's project. This collaboration typically occurs after the developer has acquired as many parcels in a redevelopment site as it can through private market transactions.

During project planning, city authorities often may have to demonstrate blight or slum conditions in the area slated for redevelopment. States allowing the use of eminent domain for blight removal generally establish criteria to determine blight. These criteria may consider conditions of blight that impose a physical or economic burden on a community.

Examples of physical blight in some state laws include buildings in which it is unsafe or unhealthy for persons to live or work. Indications of physical blight may include building code violations, structural dilapidation and deterioration, defective building design or physical construction, or faulty or inadequate utilities. Blight also may include neighboring or nearby property uses that are incompatible with one another and prevent the economic development of the respective parcels, such as the existence of irregularly sized lots. Depreciated or stagnant property values, high vacancy or turnover rates of commercial property, or increased abandonment of buildings and lots can be indications of economic blight, as can high crime rates or residential overcrowding.

While state laws often determine blight factors, authorities may have some latitude in applying them to properties and areas. The City of Chicago, following Illinois law, must apply a 13-factor test to determine blight for a redevelopment project area. To classify an entire area, such as a city block, as blighted, five or more of the factors must be clearly present and reasonably distributed throughout a project area. City officials explained that this standard means that at least a third to one half of the properties in a designated area meet at least 5 of the 13 blight factors. Officials in Los Angeles informed us that in order to adopt a redevelopment plan an area must generally be characterized by one condition of physical blight and one condition of economic blight. According to officials at the Denver Urban Renewal Authority, in order to undertake any redevelopment project, a blight designation must precede any redevelopment action. In addition, the officials explained to us that early in the project development stage, the authority conducts a study, pursuant to Colorado state statute, to determine that a minimum of 4 of the 11 blight characteristics in state law are present in the designated area. These criteria include unsanitary or unsafe conditions, deteriorated or deteriorating structures, environmental contamination, and the existence of conditions that endanger life or property.

Property Valuation Stage

The property valuation stage may involve title studies and property appraisals that city, state, or contract appraisers often conduct. Several state and city officials with whom we met or spoke described the need to conduct title studies to determine legal ownership of a property and ascertain any lien holders. To determine the fair market value of the property, which is generally the amount of the first offer made by public authorities, city officials described using an independent, certified appraiser. According to officials in New York City, fair market value is determined by valuing the highest and best use of the property on the date of acquisition. In Los Angeles, city officials explained that state law defines fair market value as the highest price that a willing buyer and willing seller would agree to, neither being compelled to buy or sell and each having full knowledge of all of the uses, and restrictions on use, to which the property may be put.[44] In other words, officials from the Los Angeles authority are required to pay owners not less than the amount for which their property would sell privately on the open market if it were unaffected by a possible eminent domain action. Massachusetts Highway Department officials described having all appraisals exceeding $175,000 in value reviewed by a real estate review board appointed by the state's transportation commissioner for accuracy and then submitted for final approval to the transportation commissioner. Some transportation authority officials also described using in-house appraisers at their agencies. During this stage, owners also may obtain appraisals of the fair market value on their property, although sometimes at their own expense.

Property Acquisition Stage

The property acquisition stage may involve a formal offer, negotiation by the city, state, or redevelopment authority officials, and at times, an impasse leading to an eminent domain filing by an authority's legal counsel. Multiple authority officials described using eminent domain after many attempts at a negotiated settlement had been unsuccessful. If the owner does not agree with an authority's initial offer, then some authorities may provide additional offers above the appraised value. In some localities, this sort of negotiation involves the owner identifying special circumstances that justify a higher level of compensation. Denver authorities told us that their initial offer to purchase is typically based on an appraisal. Any settlement that can be reached at the midpoint between the city's appraisal and the property owner's appraisal when the latter is higher is considered an appropriate settlement. The Denver official stated that it is the city's practice to pay more than the fair market value on the property to compensate for inconvenience or intangible difficulties caused by condemnation. When seeking a negotiated settlement, the authorities we contacted had different limits on the percentage amount over the appraised value that they could offer prior to invoking their power of eminent domain. For example, the Community Redevelopment Agency of Los Angeles cannot make an offer of over 120 percent of the appraised value of the property without agency board approval. A higher offer by the redevelopment agency may be considered a gift of public funds, which the agency, by law, cannot make, according to officials. In New York City, based on agency protocols, the Department of Citywide Administrative Services may pay no more than 110 percent of the original appraisal prior to the use of eminent domain. Similarly, the city's Department of Housing Preservation and Development has established rules to pay no more than 120 percent of the original appraisal prior to the use of eminent domain. In Chicago, a city official estimated that within 1 year, 75 percent of owners settle at an amount between 100 and 150 percent of the original offer.

Once authorities are certain that the owner will not settle or that the legal owner cannot be located, they may file to condemn the property with eminent domain in the appropriate court.[45] However, the manner in which authorities can invoke eminent domain differs. For example, two state DOTs we contacted have established policies to invoke eminent domain for each acquisition undertaken, including acquisitions involving willing sellers, to ensure that the authority is the sole legal title holder on the property. Multiple cities and state departments of transportation told us they also had the statutory authority to use a procedure known as "quick-take," which refers to the ability to petition a court for immediate vesting of a property's title. If the petition is granted, the court transfers the property to the authority and the final compensation is determined at a later date. The authority must deposit the estimated compensation with the court, which owners may withdraw without relinquishing their ability to argue for more compensation. Local officials have noted that for most eminent domain filings, the authority and the owner come to a settlement without the need for a trial. For instance, officials from three authorities we contacted estimated that 90 percent of all eminent domain filings were settled prior to trial.

Although few eminent domain cases go to jury trial, authority officials stated that eminent domain is the most effective tool they have to acquire needed property from owners who hold out for a higher purchase price or refuse to sell. Officials in one city explained that they also use eminent domain to void leases on property while other officials explained that they use it to obtain abandoned property when no owner can be located. For example, city officials with whom we spoke stated that eminent domain is needed to acquire properties from owners that purchase and hold on to property after an area is slated for redevelopment. Officials stated that they generally believe these owners are speculating that land values will increase because of the expected public investment in the redevelopment project.

Relocation Stage

The relocation stage may involve outreach by the condemning authority and the provision of relocation benefits by agency or contracted relocation specialists to displaced residential or commercial owners or tenants. For instance, New York City defines displaced party as any family, individual, partnership, corporation, or association that is displaced or moves from real property, or who moved his or her personal property from such real property, on or after the date of acquisition of the real property for a public improvement or urban renewal site or project.[46] The URA's definition of a "displaced person" covers anyone who moves because they received a written notice that a program or project undertaken by a federal agency or with federal financial assistance intends to acquire his or her property (including a rental property).[47]

Some authorities, such as the cities of Los Angeles and Chicago, have dedicated offices within the condemning agency to manage the provision of relocation benefits. Other localities, including New York City, sometimes contract out this responsibility to private relocation firms, for example when undertaking larger projects involving multiple displaced parties.

Multiple relocation specialists with whom we spoke, whether they were authority officials or contracted specialists, reported contacting the property owner as soon as the public entity received the authority to take the owner's specific property or soon thereafter and providing relocation support for the duration of the settlement or condemnation. For example, Chicago officials told us that within five days of the city's first offer letter, relocation specialists will contact the property owner and tenant to set-up a face-to-face interview to determine their needs. Relocation specialists may meet with displaced residents at numerous steps of the land acquisition process. They may explain the residents' rights, benefits, and obligations and may interpret legal notices received from the authority. According to some relocation specialists, residential tenants and owners are to be relocated to comparable replacement housing that is decent, safe, sanitary, and functionally equivalent to the displaced dwelling. Relocation specialists from two localities described making every effort to house residents in neighborhoods of their choice, including their current neighborhood if possible, and finding rental housing for residents who were renters. City officials from four of five cities we visited showed us new residential apartment buildings, one of which included services, such as child care and computer centers, into which they moved displaced residents.

For business occupants, relocation specialists may conduct comprehensive analyses of the business' location requirements, fixtures, moving costs, and other relevant considerations to find a comparable site for business relocation. In one city we were told that relocation specialists work with the business owners to address all commercial issues, including negotiating all comparable square footage costs and rent and getting the same phone number transferred to a new location. Some relocation specialists are associated with local retail and office landlords and attempt to negotiate a price which, combined with relocation funding under the URA, initially can keep the rental costs similar to the previous location. According to all of the relocation specialists who we interviewed, relocated commercial occupants generally have done better financially in other, more economically stable neighborhoods.

Relocation benefits under the URA and many local and state laws include some or all of the following payments to residential and commercial tenants:

- Actual moving expenses, which may include packing and moving expenses, storage of personal property, the cost of dismantling, disconnecting, and reconnecting machinery and utilities, loss of personal property caused by the move, the expense of searching for a substitute business site, moving insurance, advertising related to the move, or other related expenses (or a fixed moving allowance in some locations);
- Compensation over the acquisition cost of the property for an owner to purchase a comparable replacement home, pay increased mortgage costs, or pay closing costs;[48]
- For tenants, a monthly rental subsidy to rent a comparable dwelling for a period of 42 months that is equal to the differential between what the tenant was paying at the displaced dwelling and the payment at the comparable dwelling (many localities also allow this payment to be madein a lump sum so that renters may use it as a down payment to purchase a home); and
- A payment in lieu of moving and related expenses in nonresidential moves, which maybe made to a commercial owner when relocation would result in substantial loss of business.

USE OF EMINENT DOMAIN GENERATES BENEFITS AND COSTS AFFECTING A WIDE ARRAY OF COMMUNITY INTERESTS AND INDIVIDUALS

For selected projects where eminent domain was used that we reviewed or visited, authorities described the previous conditions of the selected areas and they told us or we observed some of the benefits realized by communities after the projects were completed. Examples of benefits to the community included increased job opportunities and modernized or safer infrastructure. Property rights groups told us about the negative effects that the use of eminent domain could have on property owners, community residents, and businesses, such as the loss of small businesses or the dispersal of residents who relied upon each other in informal networks. In addition to the losses to the community, the property rights groups noted that the manner in which authorities implement procedures for using eminent domain also affects property owners. For example, national and local property rights groups identified problems with how some authorities communicate with property owners, designate areas as blighted, and value property.

In Cases We Reviewed, Conditions of Condemned Property Varied

The use of eminent domain generates benefits and costs that could affect various parties—such as property owners, businesses, authorities, and city officials—whose interests may diverge. The great variety in benefits and costs makes it difficult to establish objective measures to examine the overall impact of projects involving eminent domain. In addition, the lack of aggregated data on the purpose and frequency of eminent domain use further limits this effort. However, for selected projects where eminent domain was used that we reviewed or visited, authorities described the previous conditions of the selected areas and they told us, or in some instances we observed, some of the benefits realized by communities after the projects were completed.

Prior to condemnation, according to local and state officials, a variety of conditions existed in selected areas in which eminent domain was used. For example, according to city officials, some of the urban areas slated for redevelopment included buildings in substandard condition. Many buildings were vacant or abandoned with few or no improvements made for multiple years; some properties had missing window glass, collapsed roofs, accumulated debris on the parcel, and other conditions that created a public health hazard. However, in some cases that we reviewed, authorities acquired occupied residences and operating businesses to redevelop an area. In one area, a building occupied by long-standing businesses providing retail services to the neighborhood was under threat of condemnation by eminent domain. Although this building was not unusually dilapidated, it was within a redevelopment area designated as blighted, and thus subject to acquisition by eminent domain.

According to local and state officials, road conditions in some projects reviewed included inadequately sized or dilapidated streets, sidewalks, or curbs. Traffic flow and access in some neighborhoods were poorly planned. For example, industrial traffic reportedly moved through residential areas in one project we reviewed. In other road or highway projects, according to state transportation officials, conditions included operable, but older roads requiring modernization, such as new interchanges to better handle traffic. Other roads required new safety features, such as turning or deceleration lanes, or straightening of tight curves in the road. We also reviewed other types of infrastructure projects, such as the New York City water tunnel previously discussed. According to city officials, the condition of the original water tunnels servicing the metropolitan area was questionable because they had not been inspected since being built in the early twentieth century.

Characteristics of Selected Redeveloped Areas Varied, with Local and State Officials Often Reporting Resulting Community Benefits

Condemned property is often redeveloped as part of a larger redevelopment or improvement project. City officials considered outcomes of these projects as benefits to the community, and emphasized that they could not have completed the projects without the use of eminent domain. However, authorities told us they often obtain much of the land for projects, including urban redevelopment projects, transportation projects, utility projects and others, through negotiated purchases and condemn a small number of the needed properties. Therefore, benefits to the community cannot be attributed solely to the use of eminent domain and are more likely the result of the redevelopment projects for which eminent domain was used.

According to local and state officials and based on some of the projects we observed, the redeveloped areas have a variety of characteristics. In urban areas, redevelopment led to additional housing stock (including affordable housing set asides), new commercial centers with additional local job opportunities, reduced crime in some areas, and modernized infrastructure. For example, in Chicago, the downtown redevelopment of a sparsely occupied block produced a 27-story municipal building, which city officials described as fully leased with retail stores and office space, including a parking garage and a mass transit station serving many parts of the city, including both airports. In New York City, the Department of Housing Preservation and Development used eminent domain to assemble land for the Melrose Commons project in the South Bronx. The agency is working with several private and nonprofit developers to construct over 3,200 affordable housing units to turn what a high-level official characterized as one of the most blighted areas in the city into a thriving neighborhood.

Officials cited benefits from transportation projects that include safer, more efficient roadways and traffic patterns. In Los Angeles, the widening of a street from two lanes to four lanes with center left turn lanes alleviated what officials described as perennial congestion, provided additional parking, and reduced accidents on a major artery in the western part of the city. Additional improvements resulting from this project included new curbs, gutters, street lighting, traffic signals, sewers, and storm drains.

City officials cited other types of improvements resulting from redevelopment, such as less contaminated land and new public green space or parks. According to Baltimore officials, sometimes vacant lots are acquired and provided to community groups for gardens. New York City officials explained that eminent domain could be an important tool to acquire brownfields in the city for remediation, although authorities there have yet to do so. Much of the 581 miles of waterfront in New York City has been contaminated in the past. According to officials, many developers are not interested in developing contaminated waterfront properties because they do not want to be liable for cleaning up the contamination. Property owners also may be unable or unwilling to sell properties that are or may be contaminated; thus, the city could acquire the properties through eminent domain, decontaminate them, and put the land to public use.

Property Owners and Groups Representing Them Reported Negative Effects on Communities from Eminent Domain Use

Property owners, property rights groups, and national community-based organizations described a number of negative effects from using eminent domain. For example, properties acquired through eminent domain may remain unused for some time, according to city officials and a property rights group. As an example, in downtown Chicago in 1989, the city condemned 16 improved, occupied buildings (one with historic landmark status the city had removed prior to condemnation) for a two-tower office and retail development. Because of a downturn in the local real estate market, the proposed project did not begin. However, according to Chicago officials, a $500 million development is now under construction on the long vacant land. In another example, Los Angeles acquired an industrially zoned parcel through eminent domain to build an animal shelter. According to city officials, to preserve the parcel for commercial use, the city is considering an alternate site for the animal shelter. As a result, the condemned property remains unused to date. In both of these instances, the cities expended public funds acquiring the land, including legal costs associated with invoking eminent domain.

Property rights groups and one national community organization further noted that certain costs to communities may not be compensated when eminent domain is used. These issues include the dispersal of residents in low-income communities to other neighborhoods or cities. The residents of low-income neighborhoods may rely on one another for day-to-day needs such as child care, according to the community organization. If these residents lose their homes through eminent domain and are relocated to new areas, then some of the resources upon which they depend also can be lost. Property rights and community groups added that owners also suffer emotional costs when losing a home. Making people leave their homes can be destabilizing to individuals or families even when relocation costs are provided.

Property rights groups also noted other community impacts, such as rent destabilization in neighborhoods affected by eminent domain and a reduction in an area's affordable housing stock when units are acquired and replaced by commercial developments. Other potential costs to the community that the groups mentioned include reductions in homeownership and the number of small businesses in an area. Furthermore, according to one property rights group, there is a tendency for cities to use eminent domain to remove manufacturing companies and replace them with retail businesses to collect increased sales revenue. However, removing manufacturing companies may have a negative effect on the community because it decreases the number of manufacturing jobs that are available.

Property Owners and Groups Representing Them Raised Concerns about the Land Acquisition and Eminent Domain Processes

The procedural requirements we previously described could provide some safeguards for property owners, such as ensuring that they receive timely public notice and just compensation. However, the effectiveness of the procedures depends on how well they are implemented by the authority invoking eminent domain. Property owners and property rights advocates we interviewed identified problems with how some authorities communicate with property owners, designate areas as blighted, and value property. Property rights advocates also expressed concern that owners may not fully comprehend the benefits available to them when an authority acquires their property.

Owners May Not Receive Public Notices and May Have Limited Opportunity to Speak at Public Hearings

Multiple owners and property rights groups with whom we met reported receiving little advanced, misleading, or no notice of public hearings or proposed condemnation actions by the relevant authority. These problems may prevent owners from voicing concerns about the proposed acquisition of their properties. For example, property rights groups in Los Angeles told us that many owners do not receive the statement of interest-owner participation letter that the authorities told us they send to all owners during the planning stage of each project. Property rights groups in Denver and New York said that notice was posted on signage, but not sent in a letter. According to the Denver group, the method of posting a notice at one site would not disseminate information about public hearings to most owners in a community. In another locality, the public notice that property owners received was reportedly not clear. For example, one authority sent a notice informing the owners of the redevelopment project and their responsibilities in a format that some owners confused with junk mail; it did not resemble an official letter. Finally, in Denver, property rights advocates told us that owners need notice earlier in the process. They said that owners learn about the condemnation after the initial planning has occurred and the urban renewal area has been designated. However, authorities in cities we visited consistently said that they always sent notice to owners of hearings—which give affected property owners multiple opportunities to voice concerns about the proposed plan and potential property acquisition—and sent notice of acquisition activities as required in all applicable laws and regulations.

Even when notice is received, owners may not have the financial or technical ability to fully comprehend what actions an authority is taking, what recourse they may have, or where to go to for assistance in understanding the proceedings or terms mentioned in the notice. For instance, one authority sent a statement of interest-owner participation letter to property owners stating that a redevelopment project was proposed for their area. The letter states that owners may, within 30 days propose their own alternative plan for redevelopment of the area. However, property rights groups explained that most owners do not have the money or skills needed to develop and execute a redevelopment plan. On the other hand, officials in this locality explained that multiple public funds and technical assistance were available to help owners formulate alternative business development plans. The letter of intent, officials said, provided the owners needed information about how to access these public benefits, remain in the community during redevelopment, and ultimately benefit from the project.

One local organization involved in urban redevelopment explained that local public hearings and the voting on proposed project plans (which may provide authorities the power to take property) by governmental bodies, such as city councils, occurred on different dates. Of concern was that the votes would happen without public attendance, thereby reducing the transparency of the process. Furthermore, a concern was raised about the time owners had to speak at hearings. In one locality, each owner was reportedly allowed only three minutes to address the elected body that would decide to approve or deny the project plan in which eminent domain might be used.[49]

To facilitate better communication between property owners and government authorities looking to assemble land, some states, such as Utah, have established a Property Rights Ombudsman's office.[50] According to the current official in Utah, the ombudsman is an attorney hired by the state as an independent source of information and assistance for property owners and others involved in the acquisition of property for public projects. The ombudsman, who provides services free of charge to owners, can mediate disputes, arrange for arbitration, order appraisals, and provide information to property owners and governmental authorities acquiring land. Connecticut and Missouri reportedly have recently adopted statutes creating property rights ombudsman-type offices.

Blight Designations May Be Broadly Construed and Affect Nonblighted Properties

Many property rights groups and owners with whom we spoke were critical of blight designation processes in their localities. They said that nonblighted property parcels may be designated blighted because of factors such as design flaws, high density, turnover of occupants, and irregularly shaped parcels. According to some property rights groups, by these criteria almost any property or area in question may be considered blighted. They felt that blight should be defined narrowly based mainly on public health and safety risks from a specific property.

According to officials from one national organization, farmland may be wrongly designated as blighted. Many farms have older and what may appear to be dilapidated homes and barns, or old storage sheds and tractors, which makes the property especially susceptible to a blight designation. The officials added, however, that these buildings and machines are often fully functional or operable, meet housing or farm needs, and pose no public danger.

In the projects we reviewed where eminent domain was used to remove blight, blight was almost always designated by area (such as a city block) rather than by parcel. Owners and property rights groups opposed to this practice stated that nonblighted property can then be taken based on this area-wide designation. During the project planning stage, usually for projects that are considered urban redevelopment or blight removal, authorities designate the physical boundaries of areas selected for redevelopment and determine the presence of blight in the area. This designation is often then applied to all parcels in the area which, in turn, allows authorities to acquire any property in the designated area. Property owners and community groups argue that not all property in such areas is blighted; rather, many properties are improved and occupied.

Furthermore, we were told that the planning stage and blight designation can occur years before an authority is able to commence acquisition and construction in the area. For example, one area we reviewed initially was deemed blighted in 1986. The blight designation, and with it the threat of eminent domain, destabilized property values in the neighborhood for nearly 20 years, according to one owner. Although the area has been an official redevelopment area since 1986, local officials told us that state redevelopment law limits a blight designation to 12 years. The authority is then required by law to return to the deciding elected body to again prove blight before the authority is able to move forward with the project.

Property rights groups also expressed concerns that blight may be exacerbated by the redevelopment activity and has been termed "developer blight"—that is, the physical decline of a parcel or area, such as a city block, once a redevelopment project has been announced. For example, in Denver, a property rights group told us that it is difficult to isolate the causes and effects of blight in their area because once an area is designated as blighted its decline might hasten. The public knowledge of the impending redevelopment and related property acquisition, according to one concerned group, can cause property values to fluctuate and discourage property owners from maintaining their dwellings or businesses or, in other words, cause an area to become blighted. In one neighborhood, according to a local property rights group, improved residential buildings were largely occupied and multiple businesses were open prior to the announcement of a redevelopment project. However, once the project was announced and the authority began the project design and planning stage, the developer purchased many of the properties and over time, failed to maintain them properly. This activity, according to the property rights group, constituted developer-initiated blight in the neighborhood. Remaining owners are concerned that "developer blight" has reduced their property values and that they will not receive what they consider just compensation from the authority as the project proceeds. Another group suggested that redevelopment plans and blight designations may prevent new businesses from relocating to a neighborhood that was revitalizing on its own because of the public's awareness that authorities will have the power to use eminent domain in the area. Authority officials told us that areas they seek for redevelopment are not revitalizing on their own, but rather declining and becoming further blighted.

Some Property Owners Claim They Received Insufficient Compensation and Others Faced High Costs to Challenge Condemnation or Compensation

While property valuation is intended to provide property owners compensation at fair market value for their property, property rights groups and owners expressed concern about the reasonableness of property appraisals. Multiple property rights groups believed that localities undervalue property and make offers lower than owners would receive on the market. One group cited large differentials between final jury awards and first appraisal amounts in cases in which owners challenged a condemnation. Owners in this property rights organization who challenged initial offers reported receiving an average of 40 percent more in compensation than the initial offer. Conversely, officials of the local authority claim that it would be to their detriment to make an unreasonably low offer at any stage in the negotiation process because an offer not in good faith might enable a jury to award additional damages to a prevailing owner.

Some believe that property is undervalued because of when appraisals take place. In New York, one owner, attempting to remain in his home, stated that if he were eventually required to sell his property, it would be appraised long after all other neighborhood owners had settled and moved away. With most of the neighborhood acquired, the owner believed that, should he lose his bid to keep his property, the value of his property would be lower than when the neighborhood was fully occupied. One state mediator of property disputes explained that an approved redevelopment area creates a hardship for owners, which is exacerbated when the project construction date is unknown. Owners in this case may have a more difficult time selling their property on the open market because it is within a redevelopment zone and subject to eminent domain. On the other hand, in one city we reviewed, buyers actively sought property in areas slated for redevelopment because the prospect of an authority acquiring the property was high.

Property rights groups also noted that property and business owners may be uninformed about the benefits provided to them once their property is taken by eminent domain. In Denver, a property rights group stated that owners did not always realize that money was available for relocation benefits. In other localities, property rights groups noted that owners might have known that some financial support was available, but might not have been aware of the range of benefits. However, property rights groups also stated that acquisition and eminent domain can cost business owners more than the amount compensated for under the URA or state and local relocation regulations. For example, the URA may often only partially cover expenses related to either lost inventory or transferring inventory to the new location. Moreover, businesses are not compensated for lost goodwill or for loss of business attributable to the new location under the URA.

Multiple property rights groups further explained that owners often are unable to fight a condemnation action if they want to retain their homes or businesses or seek additional compensation because costs related to hiring an appraiser or attorney, as well as court costs, are too high. Property rights groups believe that many owners sell their property under the threat of condemnation when they otherwise would not do so because they cannot afford to fight the action, something which can take several years.

In New York City, a contested condemnation can take more than 10 years to settle, according to city officials we interviewed. Authorities counter that, under certain circumstances, there is money available to owners to fight eminent domain. In some localities, authorities can use quick take, in which the authority obtains the title of the property and deposits the estimated compensation with the court. Owners, authorities note, can withdraw these funds to challenge the authority's valuation of their property. However, a property rights group and a state mediator emphasized that the owners cannot use these funds to dispute the authority's right to take the property. Challenges to the right to take must typically be made and heard prior to quick take procedures.[51]

According to one national organization, partial condemnations of farmland do not always result in just compensation. If authorities were to take only a portion of a farm and that portion ran directly through the middle of the property, the owner's business could be negatively affected. For example, one state reportedly developed a toll road that ran through the middle of a farm property. The farmer was paid the value of the land taken by the authority, but according to this organization, the damage done to the farm's business was not compensated. The road reduced the farm's crop yield, forced the farmer to maintain equipment on both sides of the walled toll road, and necessitated the costly alteration of an irrigation system.

SINCE JUNE 2005, MANY STATE LEGISLATURES HAVE ENACTED CHANGES TO THEIR EMINENT DOMAIN LAWS

Numerous states have adopted at least one of three general types of changes to their eminent domain laws since June 2005. In particular, some states amended their eminent domain laws and placed restrictions on the use of eminent domain for economic development, increasing tax revenues, or transferring condemned property from one private entity to another. Other states revised their eminent domain procedures or added requirements. Finally, some states defined or redefined key terms related to the use of eminent domain, such as blight or blighted property, public use, and economic development. Several states had ballot initiatives on constitutional amendments to restrict current eminent domain laws. In addition, some states, including those that did and did not enact any changes, commissioned studies on their state's eminent domain laws.

Slightly More Than Half of All State Legislatures Modified Their Eminent Domain Laws

After the Supreme Court's *Kelo* decision, 29 states enacted at least one of three general types of changes to their eminent domain laws from June 23, 2005, through July 31, 2006.[52] These changes include placing certain restrictions on the use of eminent domain, revising procedural requirements, and defining or redefining key eminent domain terms. While at least 3 of the 29 states specifically made reference to the *Kelo* decision in connection with their legislation, other states stated that the legislation was enacted to protect property rights and limit eminent domain use. Figure 3 identifies the states that enacted changes and the types of changes they enacted to their eminent domain laws.

Restrictions on Eminent Domain Use for Certain Purposes

According to our analysis, 23 of the 29 states enacted changes that placed restrictions, with certain exceptions, on the use of eminent domain for economic development, increasing tax revenues, or transferring condemned property to a private entity (see fig. 3). Specifically, some of these states prohibited the use of eminent domain to transfer private property to a private entity for economic development unless the primary purpose of the use was to eliminate blight. For example, both Alabama and Maine now prohibit condemning authorities from taking property in a nonblighted area for purposes of private retail, office, commercial, residential, or industrial development or use. In addition, Ohio imposed a moratorium, through December 31, 2006, on the use of eminent domain to take land within a nonblighted area when the purpose is economic development that leads to ownership of the property being vested in another private person. Furthermore, Florida prohibits the use of eminent domain to take private property for the purpose of preventing or eliminating slum or blight conditions.

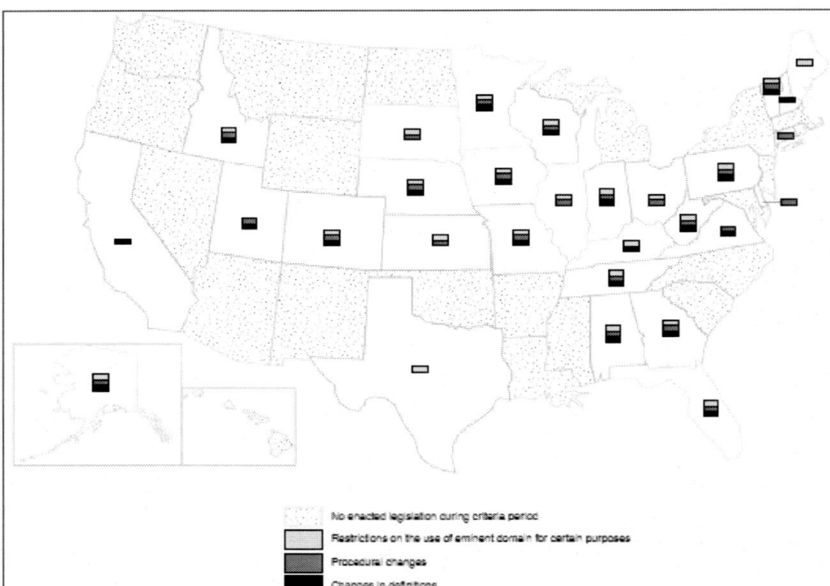

Sources: GAO (analysis); Art Explosion (map).

Figure 3. Changes to State Eminent Domain Laws from June 23, 2005, through July 31, 2006.

However, most of the states that enacted changes restricting the use of eminent domain for economic development, increasing tax revenues, or transferring condemned property to a private entity did make an allowance for the transfer of private property to a private entity for public rights of way and public utilities. Some states included other exceptions. For example, Alabama, Kansas, and Nebraska allow the use of eminent domain to clear a defective title under certain circumstances.

Procedural Changes

Twenty-four of the 29 states changed their eminent domain procedures or added new requirements (see also fig. 3). Some states placed the burden of proof on the condemning authority to show that the use is public, the taking is necessary to remove blight, or both. For example, Colorado law states that the condemning authorities must prove by a preponderance of evidence that the eminent domain taking is for a public use. Furthermore, Colorado law sets a higher standard if the purpose is to eliminate blight— requiring condemning authorities to show by clear and convincing evidence that the taking is necessary for the elimination of blight.

In addition, some of these states require condemning authorities to provide improved or additional public notice and hearings prior to condemning a property. Utah law requires that written notice be provided to the property owner of each public meeting at which a vote on the proposed taking is expected to occur and that the property owner must be given an opportunity to be heard on the proposed taking. West Virginia redefined the requirement for public notice to require a certified letter be sent to the property owner informing the owner about the public hearing and the right to an inspection to determine if the property is blighted.

Some states also passed changes requiring condemning authorities to negotiate in good faith and increase the level of compensation to be paid to owners prior to invoking eminent domain. For example, in Missouri condemning authorities are required to establish requirements for the amount of compensation, which may be more than the fair market value. Missouri law also requires condemning authorities to pay, in addition to the fair market value, a "heritage" value for certain property owned by the same family for more than 50 years, which is equal to 50 percent of the fair market value of the property. Other procedural changes enacted by some of the states include providing the former owner of a condemned property the opportunity to purchase the property if it was not used within certain period of time or for the stated purpose and requiring the use of eminent domain to be approved by a governing body.

Changes in Definitions

Twenty-one of the 29 states defined or redefined key terms related to the use of eminent domain, including blight or blighted property, public use, and economic development (see also fig. 3). In particular, some states redefined blight or blighted property to include several explicit factors, generally emphasizing factors that are detrimental to public health and safety and removing aesthetic factors, such as irregular lot size. For example, California's statutes require that for an area to be qualified for redevelopment it must be predominantly urbanized with a combination of physical and economic conditions of blight so prevalent and substantial that they can cause a serious physical and economic burden that cannot be reversed or alleviated by private enterprise or governmental action alone, or in combination with each other, without redevelopment powers and financing mechanisms. Prior California law would have allowed, as an exception to its general rule, that property subdivided into parcels with irregular shapes and inadequate sizes for proper development could also to be considered as qualifying an areas as blighted for redevelopment purposes. California amended its definition to remove this exception.

In addition, some states redefined public use to include the possession, occupation, or use of the public or government entity, public utilities, roads, and the addressing of blight conditions. For instance, Iowa defined public use to include acquisition by a public or private utility, common carrier, or airport or airport system necessary to its function. Indiana included highways, bridges, airports, ports, certified technology parks, and public utilities as public uses. Finally, some states also established that economic development—which was defined by those states to include activities to increase tax revenue, the tax base, employment, or general economic health—does not constitute public use or purpose.

Several States Had Constitutional Amendments on Fall Ballots

At least six state legislatures approved constitutional amendments on restricting current eminent domain laws, which were placed on the ballot for voter consideration.[53] For example, the Louisiana legislature approved two proposed constitutional amendments that were passed on September 30, 2006, by the voters in that state. These two amendments, among other things, (1) prohibit the taking of private property for use by or transfer to a private person; (2) limit public purposes to a list of factors, which includes such purposes as the removal of a threat to public health and safety; (3) exclude economic development, enhancement of tax revenue, and incidental benefits to the public from being considered in the determination of a public purpose; and (4) provide an option for the former owner to purchase condemned property or a portion of it should the property go unused by the authority that originally acquired the property. In addition, citizen-initiated proposals to amend the state constitution obtained the requisite number of signatures and were placed on a ballot in California, Nevada, and North Dakota.[54] For example, the Nevada Property Owners Bill of Rights initiative to amend the state constitution in regards to eminent domain qualified for the Nevada 2006 general election ballot. The amendment would, among other things, establish just compensation as the amount necessary to place owners in the same position monetarily as if property had not been taken and prohibit the direct or indirect transfer of property from one private party to another.

Some States or State Associations also Commissioned Studies on the Use of Eminent Domain

Several states and state associations also commissioned studies to determine if any changes were needed to their eminent domain laws. For example, in November 2005, the president of the New York State Bar Association appointed a special task force on eminent domain to provide legal analysis and recommendations about appropriate legislative and regulatory considerations in the practice of eminent domain law in the aftermath of the *Kelo* decision. According to a report issued by the task force, little state-specific research and data exist to accurately assess both the need for, and the impact of, changes to the state's eminent domain laws.[55] The task force suggested that the state legislature begin the collection and analysis of such data before deciding on appropriate substantive modifications to the law. For example, the report lists several questions that could be answered through empirical research, including how often condemnation proceedings are instituted and how many times eminent domain is used for economic development. Consequently, the task force recommended that a Temporary State Commission on Eminent Domain be established to further study the use of eminent domain in New York.[56]

In June 2005, the Governor of Missouri established by executive order a task force to study the use of eminent domain, including when the property being acquired by eminent domain would not be directly owned or primarily used by the general public. The task force recommended three categories of actions: redefining the scope of eminent domain, improving the procedures and process required for exercising eminent domain, and providing penalties for condemning authorities that abuse the eminent domain process.[57] As a result, the state enacted changes to its eminent domain laws in July 2006. The governor of New Mexico also issued an executive order in which he stated that the most effective method of examining *Kelo's* impact on the state's eminent domain laws and practices was by convening a task force of the state's eminent domain experts to determine what steps should be taken to ensure that condemnation would be used responsibly. Therefore, he appointed a state commission to make recommendations on eminent domain reform.

Finally, in November 2005, Ohio enacted legislation that created a task force to study the use and application of eminent domain in the state and how the *Kelo* decision affects state law governing the use of eminent domain. On August 1, 2006, the task force issued its report, which, among other things, recommended that the state retain the use of eminent domain as a tool for the elimination of blight, even if the property that is taken is converted to another private use; rewrite and tighten the definition of blight; and require that a majority of the properties in an area be blighted to designate it as such. The report also recommended (1) prohibiting eminent domain takings solely for the purpose of generating added tax revenue, (2) prohibiting declaring blight solely on the basis of additional revenue that could be generated, and (3) compensating the property owner for actual moving and relocation expenses, and, when appropriate, loss of business, goodwill, and attorney's fees.[58]

OBSERVATIONS

An inherent right of sovereignty, eminent domain is a government's power to take private property for a public use while fairly compensating the property owner. Despite its fundamental significance, little is known about the practice or extent of the use of eminent domain in the United States. The matter of eminent domain remains largely at the level of state and local governments that, in turn, delegate this power to their agencies or designated authorities. Since multiple authorities have the power to take private property within the same jurisdiction without any centralized tracking of eminent domain use, data such as the purpose for which eminent domain is used or the number of times eminent domain is used in a given locality are not readily available. The testimonial evidence we obtained from state and local authorities on the purposes for which eminent domain can be and was used generally pointed to long-established uses, such as taking land for infrastructure, particularly transportation-related projects; uses that addressed economic and social conditions, such as blight; relatively more recent uses such as environmental remediation; and initiatives aimed at promoting economic activity or community redevelopment. Recently, popular attention has concentrated on cases where the condemned land was ultimately used for economic development projects and appeared to benefit private entities. In the absence of statewide or nationwide data, it is difficult to quantify the usage of eminent domain; for example, there are no data on how frequently private-to-public or private-to-private transfer of property occurs or with what frequency eminent domain has been used by state and local governments, their agencies, or designated authorities.

Concerns and debates on the use of eminent domain for economic development purposes, as well as the *Kelo* decision, have played a role in recent state legislative activity. Many state legislatures have acted to prohibit certain eminent domain practices, such as preventing property from being transferred from one private party to another for specific purposes—for purely economic development projects, as an example. Many states changed their eminent domain laws to permit a private-toprivate transfer only if it meets certain conditions, such as the property having been determined to be blighted. Since these recent modifications to state laws have not been tested and historical data on eminent domain use are not available for comparison purposes, how these laws may affect property rights or state and local government use of eminent domain is unclear.

Our discussions with authorities and property rights groups suggest that the impact of eminent domain often depends on the nature of the project, the parties involved, costs related to legal proceedings and relocation, and the administration of procedural requirements. On the one hand, local and state government officials generally have described eminent domain as one of several tools necessary for land acquisition and explained that most of the properties assembled for projects are obtained through negotiated settlements with owners. Representatives from the authorities in cities we visited provided examples of how projects where land was assembled using eminent domain have yielded benefits to the public, including increased housing stock and new commercial centers that offer local job opportunities. On the other hand, property rights advocates described the high costs property owners faced in challenging property valuations and the intangible effects on neighborhoods when residents are involuntarily dispersed. Although we observed some of the benefits derived from the projects we visited and heard of instances in which property owners reportedly were misled by authorities about condemnation proceedings or appraisals, a lack of measures and aggregated data do not allow us to make any comment on the overall impact eminent domain has had on property owners and communities.

Regardless of their stance in the debate on eminent domain, government officials and property rights groups we interviewed identified a few concerns related to the procedures on invoking eminent domain, including the adequacy of compensation amounts and the timeliness of notification about public hearings.

First, many government officials we spoke with said that certain benefits provided under the URA, such as actual moving costs and expenses in finding a replacement site for businesses, to displaced individuals and businesses may not offer adequate compensation under certain circumstances. For example, the URA places a $10,000 cap— an amount left unchanged since 1987—on reestablishment expenses for businesses that have to relocate. A 2002 FHWA study confirmed the inadequacy of the reestablishment payments. Second, property owners and organizations advocating for property rights repeatedly told us that property owners may have limited opportunity or are unaware of the need to attend public hearings at a project's planning stage to voice their opinions about the proposed acquisition of their property. For example, some property owners and property rights groups explained that property owners may not receive public notice on a timely basis or that they may lack sufficient understanding of the legal process to be fully engaged in the hearing discussions.

To address the latter issue, at least one state has created an ombudsman office to provide information and assistance for property owners and others involved in the acquisition of property for public projects. Nevertheless, these two concerns may deserve continued attention given that just compensation and public hearings are two important safeguards designed to protect property owners.

AGENCY COMMENTS AND OUR EVALUATION

We provided a draft of this report to the Departments of Justice, Transportation and Housing and Urban Development for their review. The Department of Transportation provided technical comments, which have been incorporated where appropriate. The Departments of Justice and Housing and Urban Development did not have any comments.

William B. Shear
Director,
Financial Markets and Community Investment

APPENDIX I: OBJECTIVES, SCOPE AND METHODOLOGY

Congress, in the Transportation, Treasury, Housing and Urban Development, the Judiciary, the District of Columbia, and Independent Agencies Appropriations Act, 2006, mandated that we conduct a nationwide study on the use of eminent domain. Our objectives were to provide information on (1) the purposes and extent for which eminent domain can be and has been used; (2) the process states and select localities across the country use to acquire land, including by eminent domain; (3) how the use of eminent domain has affected individuals and communities in select localities; and (4) the changes state legislatures made to laws governing the use of eminent domain from June 2005 through July 2006.

To report on the purposes for which eminent domain has been and can be used, including the extent of its use, we reviewed pertinent sections of each state's constitution to determine whether there is a general limitation on use of eminent domain in the state for public use only. We also reviewed specific blight definitions for 10 states we selected: California, Colorado, Florida, Illinois, Massachusetts, Missouri, New York, Texas, Virginia, and Washington.[1] In addition, we interviewed multiple national associations of local and state government officials and planning professionals, national public interest groups, national property rights groups, and the National Academy of Public Administration to gain their perspective on past, current, and potential uses of eminent domain. We also interviewed federal officials from the Departments of Transportation, Housing and Urban Development, and Justice, as well as the Environmental Protection Agency, to learn about how federal programs or funding may be involved in eminent domain proceedings that state and local governments undertake. Finally, we requested information from state legislative research offices on information related to which authorities within the selected state have the authority to use eminent domain.

To learn about specific instances in which eminent domain was used, we collected project information from multiple sources. We solicited project information from 10 different national organizations that had either testified before Congress on eminent domain matters or who met the criteria laid out in our mandate for types of organizations we were expected to consult during our study. We provided these 10 organizations with a formal request for project information. Our request included basic criteria that each submitted project should meet. The criteria were: eminent domain having been used (rather than only threatened), the project being substantially completed by December 2004, the project not being primarily related to transportation, the project being located within the 10 states we selected, and preferably, that the project be funded with some federal financial assistance. In addition, we explained to the organizations that we would accept projects that did not involve federal funds, as long as the other four criteria were met.[2] We requested that each organization provide at least 5 different projects within each of the 10 states we selected for review.

In total, the 10 national organizations provided 134 projects. Based on the criteria outlined above, the desire to have at least one project in each of the selected states, and to provide a diversity of examples, we selected a total of 40 projects from the 134 for further review.[3] To obtain further information on the projects, we made at least three attempts to contact each local authority responsible for completing or overseeing the project. We completed contact with 36 of the 40 local authorities and learned that 9 of the projects did not meet our criteria because eminent domain was not used, the project was not yet complete, or the project was located in a state not included in our 10 selected states. Of the 27 remaining projects for which we were able to confirm basic project information, such as the use of eminent domain or year of completion, we sent a detailed e-mail request for project information to individuals we contacted from the local authority. Based on our conversations with the authorities responsible for the 27 projects, we scaled back the amount of information we were requesting and extended deadlines for providing the requested information. We received detailed project information for only 11 out of the 27 projects.

In addition to efforts described above, we interviewed officials from state departments of transportation of the 10 selected states. We decided to speak with these officials because interviews with national organizations and federal agencies and our literature research indicated that transportation-related projects often rely on eminent domain to assemble land. From these officials we also solicited detailed project information on transportation-related projects, mostly dealing with road improvements, construction, or expansion, in which eminent domain was used. From the state departments of transportation we received 6 projects in which eminent domain was used that also met the same criteria used to select projects provided by the 10 national organizations. We also contacted several state agencies responsible for brownfield remediation, but were unable to receive any additional projects from these agencies.

To describe how state agencies and select localities invoke eminent domain, we relied on our interviews with the 10 state departments mentioned above. We discussed the state departments of transportation's authority to invoke eminent domain, the planning phases they undertake, and their land acquisition and relocation processes. In addition, we interviewed officials from the 5 cities we visited: Baltimore, Maryland; Chicago, Illinois; Denver, Colorado; Los Angeles, California; and New York, New York.[4] During our site visits, we learned about specific projects in which eminent domain was used according to the city officials, 14 of which we toured. City officials also provided written documentation related to the selected projects that included detailed project plans, court documents, applicable state statutes and municipal codes, and relocation services provided to property owners and residents displaced due to eminent domain proceedings. Finally, we reviewed pertinent sections of each state's constitution to determine whether there is a requirement for the payment of fair or just compensation paid to the owner whose property is taken by eminent domain.

To convey how eminent domain has affected property owners and communities in select localities, we interviewed national and local organizations that advocate for property rights, in addition to property owners who claimed to have been involved in eminent domain proceedings. In accordance with long-standing GAO policy, we excluded eminent domain takings currently under litigation and, therefore, only focused on past instances involving eminent domain use. We discussed how eminent domain impacts property owners, businesses, and residents with affected owners and organizations that advocate for property rights.

To report on the changes state legislatures had made to laws governing the use of eminent domain, we reviewed legal databases and various Web-published information, such as the text or status of a bill, from state legislatures from all 50 states to determine in which states changes occurred. We then analyzed the state laws identified and grouped states based on our interpretation of those laws into three broad categories in order to more easily describe which states enacted certain types of provisions to their eminent domain laws. The three categories were: (1) states that placed restrictions on the use of eminent domain, such as prohibiting its use to increase property tax revenues, transfer condemned property to a private entity, or to assemble land for projects that are solely for economic development; (2) states that established additional procedural requirements, such as providing further public notice prior to condemnation; and (3) states that modified definitions for terms related to eminent domain use, such as blight or blighted property, public use, and economic development. We only reviewed those changes to state law that state legislatures passed and governors signed into law between June 23, 2005, and July 31, 2006.[5] Related to other state and local laws referenced in the report, we did not undertake any independent legal review of them or how those laws affect the use of eminent domain. To identify state requirements regarding eminent domain procedures, we relied on the state and local officials we interviewed and the information they provided. In the time frame allotted for our study, we could not review all pertinent state requirements regarding eminent domain authorities and procedures.

In addition to the work outlined above, we conducted an extensive literature search to assist us in meeting our objectives. Primarily, we searched for other reports, studies, and academic papers that may have tallied or assembled data sets on eminent domain use, or developed measures to assess the impact of eminent domain. To refer to or analyze data collected by others, we had to satisfy our criteria for identifying reliable and valid data, which include testing the methods and procedures others used in collecting the data. Although we identified some studies that were useful in providing us context and outlining barriers to collecting and analyzing data related to eminent domain use, we did not find any with data that met our criteria.[6] Our literature review did provide many articles, reports, and reviews of matters related to eminent domain. However, none provided an analysis of detailed data related to eminent domain use.

We conducted our work in accordance with generally accepted government auditing standards from January through November 2006 in Baltimore, Maryland; Chicago, Illinois; Denver, Colorado; Los Angeles, California; New York, New York; and Washington, D.C.

End Notes

[1] 545 U.S. 469 (2005).

[2] Pub. L. No. 109-115, div. A, title VII, § 726, 119 Stat. 2396, 2494 – 2395 (Nov. 30, 2005).

[3] For purposes of this report, we generally defined blight as a condition of a property or area that is detrimental to the physical, social, or economic well-being of a designated area. We derived this definition from our review of specific blight definitions used by 10 states—California, Colorado, Florida, Illinois, Massachusetts, Missouri, New York, Texas, Virginia, and Washington.

[4] Pub. L. No. 91-646, 84 Stat. 1894 (Jan. 2, 1971) codified at 42 U.S.C. § 4601, 4602, 4604, 4605, 4621 to 4638, and 4651 to 4655.

[5] Authorities acquire land in multiple ways, including through eminent domain. Another form of land acquisition by authorities is through negotiated settlement purchase. The steps addressed in this report that may precede the use of eminent domain also apply in cases of negotiated settlement purchase.

[6] 1-1 Nichols on Eminent Domain § 1.11 (2006); see also Mississippi & Rum River Boom Co. v. Patterson, 98 U.S. 403, 406 (1878) (eminent domain "appertains to every independent government [and] requires no constitutional recognition; it is an attribute of sovereignty").

[7] 545 U.S. 469 (2005).

[8] See Errol E. Meidinger, The "Public Uses" of Eminent Domain: History and Policy, 11 Environmental Law 1 (Fall 1980) and Jennifer M. Klemetsrud, The Use of Eminent Domain for Economic Development, 75 North Dakota Law Review 783 (1999).

[9] Pub. L. No. 91-646, 84 Stat. 1894 (Jan. 2, 1971) codified at 42 U.S.C. §§ 4601, 4602, 4604, 4605, 4621 to 4633, 4635, 4636, 4638, 4651 to 4655. For purposes of URA, federal financial assistance is defined as "a grant, loan, or contribution provided by the United States, except any federal guarantee or insurance, any interest reduction payment to an individual in connection with the purchase and occupancy of a residence by that individual, and any annual payment or capital loan to the District of Columbia." 42 U.S.C. § 4601(4).

[10] In contrast to regulatory takings—in which government regulatory actions affect private property use—eminent domain as described in this report refers to direct takings of real property, where the legal title of the property is transferred.

[11] New York City Department of Environmental Protection, New York City 2005 Drinking Water Supply and Quality Report (New York, N.Y.: 2005).

[12] According to New York City officials, although the city already owned 190 of the 407 parcels, the city needed to begin eminent domain proceedings to acquire all of the parcels to ensure that it was the sole legal title holder on the property.

[13] According to Federal Highway Administration (FHWA) officials, state DOTs have been collecting and reporting to FHWA some data related to the use of eminent domain since 1991.

[14] The numbers include instances in which state DOTs used eminent domain to acquire entire and portions of properties. The variation in the range of the number of times eminent domain was used by the state DOTs we contacted may reflect differences in state law granting state DOTs eminent domain authority, the geographic size of the state, and traffic conditions within the state, among other factors.

[15] State DOT officials also referred to these instances as "partial takings" or "strip takings."

[16] We attempted to collect information about the use of eminent domain from multiple sources, such as national organizations and cities that have used eminent domain; however, we were

unable to collect a significant amount of information on the use of eminent domain. See appendix I for more information on the methodology used to collect such information.

[17] Although multiple authorities within a state have the power of eminent domain, some may not have occasion to exercise this power.

[18] Mass Gen. Laws ch. 33, § 126.

[19] Texas Legislative Council, Fact at a Glance: Texas Statutes Granting, Prohibiting, or Restricting the Power of Eminent Domain (Austin, TX, 2006)

[20] The requirement in the Kansas Constitution for full compensation applies to corporations. However, Kansas courts have applied the federal constitutional requirement that just compensation be paid when private property is taken for public use by way of the Fourteenth Amendment's Due Process Clause. See Lone Star Industries, Inc. v. Sec. of Kansas Dept. of Transp., 671 P.2d 511, 514-515 (Kan. 1983). Further, these requirements have been codified in Kansas statutory law. Id. (citing K.S.A. 26-513(a)). New Hampshire's Constitution does not expressly mention compensation, but just compensation is nevertheless required. Thomas Tool Services, Inc. v. Town of Croydon, 761 A.2d 439, 441 (N.H. 2000) (citing Burrows v. City of Keene, 432 A.2d 15, 18 (N.H. 1981)). The North Carolina Constitution does not expressly prohibit taking private property for public use without just compensation, but its courts have inferred such a prohibition as a fundamental right integral to the "law of the land" clause that is in its constitution. Finch v. City of Durham, 384 S.E.2d 8, 14 (N.C. 1989) (citing Long v. City of Charlotte, 293 S.E.2d 101, 107- 108 (N.C. 1982)).

[21] This is also generally termed adequate compensation, due compensation, or land damages. Black's Law Dictionary (8th ed. 2004).

[22] Some authorities provide businesses with lump sum payments in lieu of those listed for all costs incurred from displacement.

[23] According to FHWA officials, while the URA provides for limits on certain relocation expenditures that are eligible for reimbursement when federal financial assistance is involved, states may be eligible for additional federal reimbursement in excess of amounts required by the URA for certain types of transportation projects.

[24] The URA permits payment for (1) actual reasonable expenses for moving, (2) actual direct losses of tangible personal property as a result of moving or discontinuing a business up to a reasonable amount that would have been required to relocate, (3) actual reasonable expenses in looking for a replacement business, and (4) actual reasonable expenses necessary to reestablish a business at a new site. 42 U.S.C. § 4622(a). However, the amount permitted to be paid for reestablishment is limited to $10,000. 42 U.S.C. § 4622(a)(4).

[25] The URA permits business and farm operations eligible for relocation benefits to elect a lump sum payment in lieu of the payments based on their actual reasonable expenses (see prior footnote). However, this payment cannot be more than $20,000. 42 U.S.C. § 4622(c).

[26] The URA designates the U.S. Department of Transportation as the lead agency, which is responsible for developing, publishing and issuing regulations implementing the URA. 42 U.S.C. § 4601(12) and 4633. The U.S. Department of Housing and Urban Development and other federal agencies funding relocation and acquisition actions actively participate in this process. 42 U.S.C. § 4633(a)(1).

[27] U.S. Department of Transportation, FHWA, Office of Real Estate Services, National Business Relocation Study, April 2002, Report No. FHWA-EP-02-030. According to FHWA officials, FHWA held two national symposia on the URA, conducted research projects, including reviews of similar laws in other countries, and held public listening sessions on regulatory and statutory reform in addition to the 2002 study.

[28] 70 Fed. Reg. 590 (Jan. 4, 2005). According to FHWA officials, one revision included re-categorizing several eligible expenses that previously counted towards the reestablishment limit set in the URA. This regulatory change, according to FHWA officials, addressed some of the concerns with the reestablishment limits by allowing additional actual, reasonable and necessary costs to be eligible for reimbursement.

[29] 42 U.S.C. § 4622(a)(4) and (c).

[30] Cal. Pub. Res. Code div. 13.

[31] N.Y. Envtl. Conserv. Law ch. 43-B, art. 8.

[32] See, for example, 735 Ill. Comp. Stat. 5/7-102.1,5/7-104, and 5/7-121.

[33] 65 Ill. Comp. Stat. 5/11-11-1.

[34] N.Y. Em. Dom. Proc. Law §§ 101, 104 and 501.

[35] Cal. Civ. Proc. Code pt. 3, tit. 7; Cal. Gov't. Code § 7260 et seq.; and Cal. Code Regs. tit. 25, § 6000 et seq. The guidelines expressly recognize the priority of federal law and that California law only applies when the federal rules are not imposed. Cal. Code Regs. tit. 25, § 6018.

[36] Cal. Code Regs. tit. 25, § 6002.

[37] Colo. Rev. Stat. § 31-25-101 et seq. (urban renewal) and Colo. Rev. Stat. 38-1-101 et seq. (eminent domain).

[38] See, for example, Md. Code Ann., Real Property § 12-206; N.Y. Gen. Mun. Law § 74- b; and Wash. Rev. Code § 8.26.065.

[39] New York City Charter § 197-c.

[40] 28 RCNY § 18-04.

[41] Pub. L. No. 109-59, § 6001(a),119 Stat. 1144, 1851 (Aug. 10, 2005).

[42] 23 U.S.C. § 135(f)(3).

[43] 23 U.S.C. § 135(g)(3).

[44] Cal. Civ. Proc. Code § 1263.320(a).

[45] Prior to an authority filing in court to condemn a property, owners may have negotiated with authorities under the threat of eminent domain. Once the authority files to condemn a property through eminent domain, the threat of eminent domain becomes the actual use of the tool. Nevertheless, owners and authorities may still continue to negotiate.

[46] 28 RCNY 18-04(b).

[47] 42 U.S.C. § 4601(6)(A).

[48] The URA limits this payment to $22,500. 42 U.S.C. §4623(a)(1).

[49] Officials from the National Academy of Public Administration told us that academy panels generally encourage improved communication between government agencies and the public and have put forth six principles of effective consultation. These include having an inclusive and well-known process, stakeholders being assisted to participate effectively, two-way exchange of information, timely access to decision makers and feedback to stakeholders, stakeholder satisfaction with the process, and stakeholder influence on results.

[50] Utah Code Ann. § 13-42-101-206.

[51] 7-2 Nichols on Eminent Domain § 2.04 (2006).

[52] The period of our analysis was from June 23, 2005, through July 31, 2006. We chose June 23, 2005, as the start date because the U.S. Supreme Court decided Kelo on this date. During our analysis period, 21 states did not make any changes to their eminent domain laws.

[53] In addition to changing their eminent domain laws, Florida, Georgia, and New Hampshire also approved a constitutional amendment further restricting eminent domain laws that was placed on the states' ballots for voter consideration. Michigan and South Carolina also had ballot measures related to eminent domain. Some other states had measures on their ballots

regarding their eminent domain statutory laws, which we did not review because they were outside our period of analysis. According to each Secretary of State's website, the proposed constitutional amendment was approved in Florida, Georgia, Louisiana, Michigan, Nevada, New Hampshire, North Dakota, and South Carolina.

[54] The California initiative approved for the ballot during the November 2006 election, if passed, would have, among other things, amended the state constitution to bar state and local governments from condemning private property and transferring it to another private party unless the transfer occurred under circumstances where the private party would perform a public use project. The California initiative failed. California's state legislature also enacted changes to its definition of blight, as noted in figure 2.

[55] New York State Bar Association, New York State Bar Association Special Task Force on Eminent Domain, New York State Bar Association Special Task Force on Eminent Domain Report (Mar. 2006).

[56] Id. at 52.

[57] State of Missouri, Missouri Eminent Domain Task Force, Final Report and Recommendations of the Missouri Eminent Domain Task Force (Jefferson City, Mo.: Dec. 30, 2005).

[58] Ohio General Assembly, Legislative Task Force to Study Eminent Domain and Its Use and Application in the State, Final Report of the Task Force to Study Eminent Domain (Columbus, Ohio: Aug. 1, 2006). Indiana also commissioned a task force to study eminent domain on May 6, 2005, which was prior to the date of the Kelo decision. See Indiana HEA 1063-2005 (P.L. 173-2005), and other states may have formed various groups, commissions or task forces to study eminent domain.

End Notes for Appendix I

[1] We selected 10 different states based on the 10 regions used by the U.S. Department of Housing and Urban Development (HUD) in its quarterly report on the nation's housing market to provide geographic diversity among the selected states. HUD's regional framework was used because HUD has established programs (e.g., Community Development Block Grant Program) to provide states and localities funds for promoting community and economic development. From the 10 regions, we selected the state in each region with the highest number of housing units (single and multifamily) authorized by building permits in 2003, 2004, and 2005 based on HUD data.

[2] We had anticipated gaining additional knowledge about projects from federal agencies, departments, and programs that may have offered some assistance to the selected projects. However, recognizing that not all projects selected may involve federal financial assistance and that our mandate focused on state and local use of eminent domain, we did not want to exclude any projects solely because federal resources were not used in the project.

[3] We selected 40 projects from the 134 received because project information provided was not always sufficient for us to determine whether to include a project in our review. For example, 27 percent, or 36 out of the 134, of the projects were either still in progress or the completion date was unknown, according to the organization providing the project information.

[4] To make effective use of time and resources, we first visited Baltimore, Maryland, to gain some perspective on redevelopment projects that involved eminent domain use. Unable to take into consideration the frequency of eminent domain use or generate a list of projects in

which eminent domain was used by state or localities, we visited the four remaining cities based on geographic diversity, location within our 10 selected states, and availability of time and resources.

[5] The period covers approximately 1 year after the Kelo decision.

[6] In addition to time and resource constraints, the lack of any systematic data that met our criteria prohibited us from performing other types of analyses. For example, we did not undertake any cost-benefit analyses of specific projects or purposes, since no data existed that quantified the various costs and benefits attributed to the various parties involved in an eminent domain taking. Also, we could not undertake a case study approach, primarily because the various involved parties could not be readily located, such as property owners who had moved due to the eminent domain taking.

In: Eminent Domain
Editor: Irene Hines
ISBN: 978-1-63483-440-7

Chapter 2

THE CIVIL RIGHTS IMPLICATIONS OF EMINENT DOMAIN ABUSE*

U.S. Commission on Civil Rights

EXECUTIVE SUMMARY

The Fifth Amendment to the U.S. Constitution states that government shall not take private property except for "public use" and with "just compensation."[1] In *Berman v. Parker*,[2] the Supreme Court held that eliminating blight qualifies as a permissible "public use" under the Fifth Amendment. In so doing, the *Berman* Court permitted Washington, DC, to take a department store that was not itself in poor condition and to transfer it to a private development corporation for the purpose of curing blight in the surrounding neighborhood, in which most of the residences were considered uninhabitable and beyond repair. Pursuant to that decision, the District of Columbia was able to expel some 5,000 low-income blacks from their homes in the name of "urban renewal."[3] Critics argue that the decision opened the door to the use (or abuse) of eminent domain by expanding the term "public use" to mean "public purpose"— an interpretation that they believe has no constitutional basis.

Subsequent to the *Berman* decision, state court decisions invoked "public use" broadly. They concluded that possible "public benefits" from increased

* This is an edited, reformatted and augmented version of a briefing report issued June 2014.

tax revenues or job creation, which could flow from a more desirable private owner (such as a large business), justified the transfer of private property from one owner to another through eminent domain, regardless of the property's condition.[4]

Some civil rights advocates have argued that local governments historically used the urban renewal condemnations *Berman* permitted to target racial and ethnic minorities. "Indeed, the displacement of African Americans and urban renewal projects were so intertwined that 'urban renewal' was often referred to as 'Negro removal.'"[5] Too often, "blight," a facially-neutral word, masked the discriminatory motives behind certain takings.[6] Today, some critics claim that officials often declare areas blighted and, therefore, in need of redevelopment that are not actually blighted, and the owners seldom receive just compensation. Critics also charge that the burden falls disproportionately on those lacking the money, political power, and influence needed to rebuff attempted takings, with the "deck stacked against" property owners.

In 2005, the Supreme Court affirmed its broad interpretation of "public use" in *Kelo v. City of New London.*[7] A divided (5-4) Court upheld the use of eminent domain by local governments to take individuals' private property and transfer it to others for the purpose of private economic redevelopment. It concluded that private economic development, similarly to the construction of roads, bridges, parks, public buildings, or other infrastructure, qualified as a permissible "public use."

In their separate dissents in *Kelo*, Justices O'Connor and Thomas derided the majority's understanding of the concept of "public use" and predicted that communities with less power than the business interests seeking their property would be disproportionately harmed by eminent domain abuse.[8] A 2007 study commissioned by the Institute for Justice, *Victimizing the Vulnerable: The Demographics of Eminent Domain Abuse,* appears to confirm the Justices' concerns, finding a disparate impact on the communities least capable of defending themselves against takings. "Taken together, more residents in areas targeted by eminent domain—as compared to those in surrounding communities—are ethnic or racial minorities, have completed significantly less education, live on significantly less income, and significantly more of them live at or below the federal poverty line."[9]

On August 12, 2011, the U.S. Commission on Civil Rights convened a briefing to discuss these issues. The bipartisan agency sought and invited speakers of varying perspectives, including scholars knowledgeable about the history of eminent domain abuse, its impact on poor and minority communities, and any implications for civil rights; federal or state legislators who had exerted effort to curb the practice; and representatives knowledgeable about allegations of eminent domain abuse in particular localities.

At the time of the briefing, 43[10] states had enacted laws attempting to limit the scope of eminent domain power sanctioned by *Kelo*, but some scholars argue that those laws contain loopholes that "continue to permit the exact same kinds of condemnations under the guise of alleviating 'blight'—a concept defined so broadly that virtually any property the government covets can be declared 'blighted.'"[11]

SUMMARY OF PROCEEDINGS

Four panelists spoke at the briefing: Ilya Somin, now Professor of Law, George Mason Law School; J. Peter Byrne, Professor of Law, Georgetown University Law Center; Hilary O. Shelton, Director, NAACP Washington Bureau and Senior Vice President for Advocacy and Policy; and David Beito, Chair of the U.S. Commission on Civil Rights' Alabama State Advisory Committee and Professor at the University of Alabama.

These panelists fielded questions from the Commissioners dealing with several issues: 1) the compatibility of or tension between the protection of individual rights and powers delegated to the states; 2) whether redevelopment projects using eminent domain disproportionately harm minority property owners; 3) whether greater government constraint on eminent domain takings, particularly those for redevelopment that transfer the property to private entities, is necessary to protect poor or politically-weak property owners who are often members of minority groups; 4) whether developers have alternative methods and can amass large sites and more successfully redevelop areas without using eminent domain (and public funding), and with less-harmful effects on displaced property owners, particularly minorities; 5) whether recent changes, such as minorities' increased political participation in the last 30 years and/or requirements for more transparency and community involvement in eminent domain procedures, have led to less eminent domain abuse; 6) whether eminent domain requirements should provide compensation for displaced businesses and tenants, not just homeowners; and 7) whether eminent domain suits have included charges of civil rights violations.

Panelist Presentations

Ilya Somin

Professor Somin said that the ownership of private property is central in our Constitution's system of liberty.[1] The public use clause of the Fifth Amendment and many similar state constitutional clauses, he said, allow the condemnation and taking of private property only if the land is for a public use. However, whether "public use" means government or general public use, or merely anything that might benefit the public, is a longstanding debate. In the founding era, jurists and commentators rarely discussed the meaning of "public use," although most understood that the Constitution barred takings that transferred property from one private individual to another unless there was a right of access to the condemned property by the general public.[2] The issue arose more in the 1860s, when property ownership was key in the conception of civil rights that led Congress to enact the Fourteenth Amendment, and in the intended guarantees of similar rights to African Americans and other minorities. This amendment, Professor Somin said, applied the public use clause and Bill of Rights to state and local governments, the entities that implement most takings.[3] According to him, Congress intended it to protect the property rights of African Americans and southern white Union supporters from state governments' threats of deprivations of property. Professor Somin said his research on this era shows that the majority of state supreme courts and most eminent domain experts took the view that "public use" meant government or general public use, not merely something beneficial to the public.[4]

In contrast, Professor Somin said, in recent decades many courts and legislatures have afforded property rights much weaker protection, even relative to other individual constitutional rights. In particular, Supreme Court cases—the 1954 *Berman* case and the more recent *Kelo* one—treated "public use" as almost any potential public benefit, without requiring proof that it is achievable.[5] Interpreting "public use" to allow state and local governments to condemn property for any reason does not make sense, Professor Somin argued, because the Fourteenth Amendment constrained state and local governments to prevent abuse. Furthermore, the Supreme Court has not been similarly deferential to governmental entities regarding the scope of other individual rights enumerated in the Constitution.[6]

According to Professor Somin, the Supreme Court's and lower federal courts' weakening protections of property rights against takings diminished the economic and social well-being of many Americans, displacing hundreds of thousands since World War II. According to Professor Somin, the majority suffering from blight condemnations and economic development takings were racial and ethnic minorities, mostly poor African Americans or Hispanics. Yet, as disproportionate victimization of minorities continued across decades, the motives for the takings changed. Professor Somin stated that during the 1950s and 1960s, urban renewal takings showed blatant prejudice against minorities, but today it is rarely evident.[7] Instead, he believes that local governments often target poor urban minorities for such condemnations because of their political weakness, which stems partly from the past discrimination these groups have suffered. Furthermore, Professor Somin said that, although the governing entities financially compensate most of the displaced property owners, they rarely, if ever, fully cover their losses, leaving the victims of eminent domain worse off than before.[8]

Some people claim that blight and economic development takings benefit rather than harm the minority poor because they promote economic growth of the community, an argument Professor Somin described as "overstated."[9] First, he believes that such condemnations often destroy far more economic assets— businesses, schools, homes, and community networks—than they create. Second, when private development is likely to produce more growth than it displaces, developers can realize market advantages without resorting to eminent domain to acquire the property and will have better results.[10]

Professor Somin said that respect for property rights helps drive economic growth. Recent research suggests that people in areas that respect property rights are more secure in their homes and businesses and invest more, which promotes economic growth. Unconstrained government intervention in property rights has the opposite effect, Professor Somin said.[11] Although economic growth and the removal of blight are both important, Professor Somin argued against destroying a community to save it from blight, recommending instead more humane and effective methods that do not forcibly displace large numbers of people.[12]

Since the Supreme Court's 2005 *Kelo* decision, 43 states enacted eminent domain reform legislation.[13] Yet, according to Professor Somin, the new laws fail to overcome eminent domain abuse because the majority of them have little effect. While they ban economic development takings, they allow takings as "blight condemnations" with such broad definitions that nearly any area qualifies.[14] He described downtown Las Vegas and Times Square in New York City as examples. In states that limit the definition of blight, the minority poor are still disproportionately at risk because many of them live in communities that meet such terms.[15] Only four states completely ban blight condemnations, securing the rights of the poor against these takings. In Professor Somin's assessment, since *Kelo*, proponents of restraint on eminent domain have raised public awareness of the issue but must work further to guarantee constitutional property rights to all Americans, particularly the most vulnerable, such as the minority poor.[16]

J. Peter Byrne

Professor Byrne stated that eminent domain empowers the government to acquire property in specific locations so that it can assemble large tracts and construct business communities, particularly when private owners refuse to sell, or hold out for excessive payment. Governments have exercised eminent domain throughout the world since Roman times.[17] Our Constitution protects owners, he claimed. It requires the government to justly compensate them for the land. He agreed with Professor Somin that the meaning of the Fifth Amendment takings clause relating to public use is controversial; yet, according to Professor Byrne, "no ... Supreme Court decision contradicts the holding of *Kelo* that 'public use' includes publicly approved condemnations for economic redevelopment of economically distressed areas." The quality of the redevelopment varies, he said, but the Ferry Building in San Francisco and Times Square in New York City are among recent successful projects.[18]

In contrast to Professor Somin, Professor Byrne stated that the use of eminent domain for economic development neither unfairly nor disproportionately harms racial and ethnic minorities. Professor Somin's remedy, which Professor Byrne described as prohibiting all use of eminent domain for economic development, including the elimination of blight, is unnecessary. Claims that eminent domain unfairly harms minorities, Professor Byrne said, arise not from today's experiences, but from urban renewal efforts before the 1960s, when publicly-funded projects bulldozed homes of many African Americans and others in failed attempts to modernize cities.[19] He suggested that Clarence Thomas's dissent in *Kelo v. City of New London* relied on this faulty argument about harm to minorities and the poor. Today, Professor Byrne said, eminent domain is valuable in redevelopment projects designed to maintain the economic competitiveness and viability of urban areas, where property ownership is fragmented and where, coincidentally, minorities live in large numbers.[20]

Political realities have changed today so that the discrimination in urban renewal projects of the 1940s and 1950s is no longer evident, Professor Byrne said. First, urban minorities such as African Americans grew in number and power. They amassed political power in nearly every U.S. city and are more influential in private real estate markets. Second, federal and local governments' fiscal relations changed. Federal money and direction diminished and local governments took control of redevelopment projects, he said, associating this with the lessening of racial biases.[21] Third, eminent domain is rarely invoked for residential properties today because local officials want to avoid the resulting negative publicity and expensive litigation. Furthermore, many federal and state statutes increased the payments due property owners beyond what "just compensation" requires. Lastly, today the application of eminent domain must meet requirements for the political consent and involvement of the community, Professor Byrne said. The rare condemnation of homes today shows little or no identifiable ethnic or racial character, he concluded.[22]

Professor Byrne further argued that economic revitalization of urban areas aids poor minorities who disproportionately dwell in cities because it increases employment and tax revenues, and hence education and city services. Without such eminent domain, large-scale development projects can occur only on greenfield sites on the edges of cities, exacerbating urban sprawl and pushing new employment opportunities further from where urban minorities live.[23]

Professor Byrne stated that changes in the political climate of economic development are evident in contrasting urban renewal in Southwest Washington, DC, in the 1950s (which the Supreme Court approved in *Berman v. Parker*), with condemnations there today. In the 1950s, the District of Columbia did not have an *elected* local government, nor any representation in Congress. Congress enacted the statute authorizing the project, and federal representatives appointed members of the redevelopment agency that executed it. Condemnations, bulldozing, and reconstruction ensued with poor African American residents suffering disproportionate displacement.[24] The most controversial recent exercise of eminent domain in Washington, DC, was the condemnation of stores in the Skyland strip mall in Anacostia for construction of a private supermarket that an under-served community needed badly.[25] Although some owners contested this action in court, many local community members supported it. Mayor Anthony Williams and the DC Council, with African Americans comprising the majority of its members, approved the project. According to Professor Byrne, although this eminent domain use in Anacostia conveyed land to a private developer and is the type of condemnation that concerns Professor Somin, the case does not present a civil rights issue appropriate for the U.S. Commission on Civil Rights' consideration.[26]

Professor Byrne further stated that condemnations for economic development cause no more harm to minorities than those for traditional public uses. In his view, government has the same incentive as private developers to seek inexpensive land for projects regardless of the intended use. For example, the government owned the sites and built highways and public housing in many brutal condemnations during the urban renewal period. At the same time, the recent Dudley Street Neighborhood Initiative in Boston used eminent domain to assemble land for affordable housing projects without giving rise to any civil rights issues.[27]

Professor Byrne suggested that the proponents of restraints on eminent domain usage focus on prohibiting it for economic development that could aid low-income people. In his view, they ignore abuses for highway construction and other public projects that have historically caused the greatest harm to minorities.[28] Professor Byrne stated that legislation recently introduced in Congress[29] is an example, adding that the bill protects speculative ownership of vacant land, but offers no safeguards for residents.[30]

According to Professor Byrne, libertarians advocate against eminent domain, and, while he respects their basic principle of valuing private property more highly than local democracy, he questions evidence used in support of their positions, such as an Institute for Justice report titled "Victimizing the Vulnerable,"[31] which he said presented "ambiguous data" and used "highly colored language." The study, he said, shows only that communities more often pursue redevelopment in poor areas than in more affluent ones.[32] It neither reveals which properties the municipalities took, nor the property owners' races. It fails to consider the scope or character of citizen participation in the decision-making, the public benefits growing out of the projects, or the distribution of those benefits. Despite these shortcomings, the study concludes that prohibiting private developers' use of eminent domain is the only way to protect the constitutional rights of all citizens, Professor Byrne said. Thus, libertarians equally oppose condemnation of property owned by large corporations and by marginal minorities, Professor Byrne said, suggesting that they use sympathy for the latter group to gain support for constraining legislative power over private property to benefit the former.[33]

One could more directly remedy the disproportionate impacts of eminent domain on poor minorities, Professor Byrne averred, by: (1) providing more procedural protections or compensation to residents than to commercial property owners; (2) mandating minimum payments to tenants, who now receive no compensation when rental housing is condemned and they are forced to move; or (3) amending the Fair Housing Act to clarify its application of condemning residences without regard to intent.[34] Professor Byrne concluded that, with today's growing economic inequality and cuts in benefits and services, many other issues are more important than any ill effects of eminent domain on minorities.[35]

Hilary Shelton

Mr. Shelton said that the NAACP, which he represents, is our nation's oldest and largest, most widely recognized grass roots civil rights organization. With branches in every state, it has about 2,200 units throughout the country. The NAACP Washington Bureau is the organization's federal legislative and national public policy arm.[36]

Too many elected and appointed officials disregard the rights and concerns of racial- and ethnic-minority Americans, Mr. Shelton said, and disproportionately misuse eminent domain against them and the economically disadvantaged, in keeping with "our nation's sad history of racial prejudice, racism, [and] bigotry." Mr. Shelton stated that authorities agree that the exercise of eminent domain affects African Americans disproportionately, although accurate, nationwide counts of those displaced are lacking, he said.[37] Mr. Shelton cited statistics from two studies. One[38] estimates that, since World War II, urban renewal takings displaced three to four million Americans from their homes, the majority of whom were racial and ethnic minorities. The other study,[39] according to Mr. Shelton, reports that, between 1949 and 1973, government officials executed 2,532 projects in 992 cities, displacing one million people, two-thirds of whom were African Americans. Eminent domain use displaced African Americans five times more often than their representation in the nation's population, he reported.[40]

Mr. Shelton explained the NAACP's concern that the U.S. Supreme Court permitted expanded use of eminent domain with its 2005 ruling in *Kelo v. City of New London*. This decision allows the government to take property by asserting that it can put the land to a higher use. This new sanction, Mr. Shelton said, fosters more discrimination. It occurs because property and community stability are more easily transferred from those with fewer resources to those with more.[41]

Mr. Shelton gave several reasons for the disparities in eminent domain displacements. First, municipalities typically pursue redevelopment projects in areas with low property values because the condemning authority pays less compensation and the state or local government realizes greater financial gains from ensuing increases in property values. Second, officials more easily accomplish eminent domain takings in low-income and predominantly racial-

and ethnic-minority neighborhoods because such residents frequently lack the resources to contest the condemnations politically or in court.[42] In addition, he reported, many believe that governing officials have aimed displacements to segregate and maintain the isolation of poor racial and ethnic minorities. Even if one dismisses segregation as a motivation, Mr. Shelton stated that, with the *Kelo* holding allowing municipalities to pursue eminent domain for private development, financial advantages compel local authorities to perpetuate and possibly exacerbate the disparate impact of eminent domain use on minority groups and the economically disadvantaged.[43]

Mr. Shelton further asserted that the exercise of eminent domain affects racial and ethnic minorities more often and more profoundly. First, the term "just compensation" in eminent domain cases is a misnomer because the market usually undervalues or has yet to recognize the worth of any property that local authorities have designated for economic development.[44] Moreover, when local governments use economic development to increase an area's tax base, the low-income families that such takings displace cannot afford to live in the revitalized communities. At the same time, any remaining affordable housing in the area increases in value.[45] A mid-1980s study[46] found that 86 percent of those relocated as a result of the use of eminent domain were paying more rent—averaging almost double the amount—at their new residences, Mr. Shelton said.[47]

Mr. Shelton indicated that destabilization of organized minority communities will likely result when local governments exercise the takings clause in areas with significant racial and ethnic populations. The dispersion of relocated minority families undermines their community support mechanisms, weakens community leaders' existing political power, and hinders efforts to further build community strength.[48] The threat of such takings undermines efforts—financial and otherwise—to build up these communities. According to Mr. Shelton, too many communities—racial and ethnic minorities, the elderly, and those with low incomes—have witnessed an often devastating abuse of eminent domain powers.[49]

On behalf of the NAACP, Mr. Shelton urged that legislators, administrators, and others listen to concerns about eminent domain abuse, hear the voices of "segments of our population that have too long been muted,"[50] and learn how eminent domain use for economic development or removal of blight exploits these communities. He added that the NAACP has concerns that eminent domain imposed for any purpose, including traditional public uses for highways, utilities, and waste disposal, disproportionately burdens communities with the least political power: the poor, racial and ethnic minorities, and working-class families. Furthermore, not just owners, but renters—both residents and small-business proprietors—suffer from the use of eminent domain and seldom receive any protections or payments.[51]

Mr. Shelton explained that the application of eminent domain must require processes that protect racial and ethnic minorities and low-income communities. He recommended to legislators and administrators that these procedures: (1) be open and transparent and guarantee the full participation of any affected communities; (2) provide fair compensation covering replacement costs for the takings, not just the appraisal value, so that those displaced are not worse off; and (3) ensure compensation for business losses on the basis of the length of time an enterprise has been located there.[52] According to Mr. Shelton, NAACP's supporters believe that all American communities deserve these protections. In conclusion, Mr. Shelton offered that, "the NAACP stands ready to work with the federal, state, and local municipal officials to develop policy and legislation to end eminent domain abuse."[53]

David Beito

Professor Beito commented that the Commission's Alabama Advisory Committee unanimously voted to pursue the issue of eminent domain abuse, which appealed to both Democrats and Republicans, but also to blacks and whites alike.[54] Nonetheless, he stated that he was speaking for himself at the briefing, not in his capacity as chair of the Alabama Advisory Committee, even as he described this committee's work.[55]

Professor Beito described a state law that, in his view, threatens the property rights of the poor and vulnerable. The Alabama Advisory Committee held two public forums on the issue, which Professor Beito called "eminent domain through the back door."[56] In 2008, witnesses at a Birmingham meeting recounted instances of blacks, particularly in the City of Montgomery, who were losing their property through application of section 11-53B-1, *et. seq.,* of the Alabama Code. Professor Beito explained that this provision allows the taking of property outside of conventional eminent domain if a local government deems a property structure blighted or a nuisance, but the section provides property owners no right to compensation.[57] The city typically declares the property a nuisance then demolishes the structure and bills the owner for the cost of demolition and removal of the rubble, often by placing a lien on the property. Because owners are often poor, many cannot afford to pay and, thus, sell or abandon their property. Professor Beito reported that most complaints about this application of eminent domain came from Montgomery, Alabama.[58]

Professor Beito exhibited several slides during his presentation. The first slide presented a Frederick Douglass quote,[59] which Professor Beito believed illustrates historical concern for property rights and serves as a model today for protecting property rights regardless of economic class. The second slide depicted a developer's demolitions through section 11-53B-1 in Montgomery in a one-year period, with a heavy concentration in black areas of the city.[60] The remaining slides were pictures of the Montgomery residences of Jimmy McCall and Karen Jones, homes which the City later demolished under section 11-53B-1.[61]

Professor Beito said Jimmy McCall described his efforts to protect his home at the second Alabama Advisory Committee forum, held in Montgomery. Mr. McCall had purchased two acres on a major thoroughfare and begun constructing his home incrementally using rare wood and other materials from his salvage operations.[62] Professor Beito said the city showed unremitting hostility from the outset, citing Mr. McCall for keeping building materials on his property, even though they were not visible from the road, and, in 2007, charging him on the grounds that his home was a nuisance. In Mr. McCall's view, he *was* fighting blight by building a new home in an under-developed area, but he suspected that wealthy developers were trying to obtain the property.[63] In 2008, Mr. McCall's attorney negotiated a court-enforced agreement allowing him 18 months to complete the home, but only a month later the city demolished the structure. Local officials obtained a court order authorizing them to raze the home and bulldozed it without giving Mr. McCall notice. When Mr. McCall contacted the judge who had allowed the demolition, she stated that she had been misled and ordered the city to pay compensation, Professor Beito related. The City of Montgomery appealed and has not yet paid Mr. McCall. Professor Beito noted that Mr. McCall fears the city will drag out its appeal until he can no longer afford to fight it.[64]

Professor Beito also described circumstances regarding Karen Jones' home. City authorities charged that the property was a nuisance because the porch was in disrepair. The city failed to inform Ms. Jones before it bulldozed the home because it continued to recognize her grandmother, deceased in 1989, as the property owner, even though Ms. Jones had documents supporting her ownership and paid the property taxes. In 2010, the city demolished the home and personal belongings it contained.[65] In May 2011, the city offered the property at auction, still naming the deceased grandmother as owner. Professor Beito then showed a video relating much of the same information about Ms. Jones' and Mr. McCall's situations.[66]

DISCUSSION

Commissioner Kirsanow said people of many ideological perspectives have been concerned about the use of eminent domain, both before and since *Kelo*. He asked Professor Somin whether allowing state and local governments to determine what constitutes a public use engenders tension between the Tenth Amendment[67] and Fifth Amendment.[68] If so, he asked, should law honor the individual property rights the Fifth Amendment protects over Tenth Amendment concerns?[69] In response, Professor Somin did not perceive any tension because the Tenth Amendment says states and the people retain the powers that the Constitution does not delegate to the federal government. Federal courts have the power to enforce any individual rights protected by the Constitution, including its Fifth Amendment. The Tenth Amendment does not prevent this federal enforcement.[70]

Commissioner Kirsanow further queried when or which case transformed the notion of what constitutes "public use" into "a public benefit." Professor Somin said that people argued for a public benefit interpretation in state courts in the nineteenth century, although only a minority of state supreme courts held that at that time.[71] The federal Supreme Court adopted "public benefit" as an interpretation of the public use clause of the Fifth Amendment in the *Berman v. Parker* case in 1954. Professor Somin added that some early 20th century and late 19th century cases were deferential to eminent domain, but did not address the public use clause of the Fifth Amendment. In that period, the Supreme Court had not yet taken the view that the Bill of Rights was incorporated against the states. Thus, one could only challenge a state taking in a federal court under the due process clause of the Fourteenth Amendment. Although the Supreme Court used a fairly deferential approach under that clause, the Court was less deferential than in *Berman* and *Kelo*. In the rare challenges to federal government condemnations that went to federal court during that period, such as an 1896 *Gettysburg* case,[72] the Supreme Court made clear that takings that transfer property to a private individual require greater scrutiny.[73] The Supreme Court's claim in *Kelo* that 100 years of precedent backed their position fosters misunderstanding, Professor Somin said. The precedent began only with *Berman* in 1954. Every case the Supreme Court cited before then was a substantive due process case under the Fourteenth Amendment and did not involve the public use clause of the Fifth Amendment.[74]

Before posing questions, Commissioner Yaki expressed concern that the briefing's title was conclusory; asserting that eminent domain abuse in fact violates civil rights. Furthermore, in the video presented by Professor Beito, the panelist stated that the "Commission" calls the narratives' examples "eminent domain abuse." Commissioner Yaki said that the Commission had not yet drawn such a conclusion. Professor Beito agreed that he misstated this in the video and clarified that the Alabama state advisory committee, and not the U.S. Commission on Civil Rights as a whole, agreed that the incidents were abuse. In addition, Commissioner Yaki suggested that the briefing did not balance opposing views about whether or not applications of eminent domain abused the civil rights of minorities.[75] Professor Beito responded that the officials who had exercised eminent domain in Montgomery, Alabama, were invited to speak at the Commission's briefing, but turned down the opportunity.[76] Later during the discussion, Commissioner Yaki suggested that the Commission should use its subpoena powers to compel testimony from Alabama officials who have elected to remain silent on this topic.[77]

Commissioner Yaki then asserted that eminent domain is not evil in itself. He knew of past abuses, but attributed them to the 1950s or early 1960s—a period before the Civil Rights Act of 1964, the Voting Rights Act, and the redistricting one-person-one-vote cases that helped minorities gain political power.[78] As a former government official involved in the use of eminent domain, Commissioner Yaki knew of a San Francisco neighborhood where redevelopment caused relocation and uprooting, but also led to increases in jobs and economic growth, and a now thriving African American community. He suggested that abuses in eminent domain could be addressed, without doing away with it.[79]

Commissioner Yaki asked Professor Byrne and Mr. Shelton whether changes in the last 30 years protect minority or disempowered communities against uprooting or relocation.[80] Professor Byrne agreed that changes in recent decades do help protect against the harm that use of eminent domain causes. In the past, Professor Byrne explained, urban renewal programs allowed mayors to work with federal agencies and bypass local political processes. The mayor controlled special local government entities that received the federal funding and could, therefore, pursue projects without citizenry influences, he said, citing New Haven, Connecticut, as an example.[81] Today, Professor Byrne said, minority groups in some communities may have less political power than those in San Francisco; however, elected city officials are wary of taking homes and strive to avoid the "political firestorm" that ensues should anyone infer ethnic or racial bias. Abuse of eminent domain in contemporary cities is now rare because the projects use local funding, not a federal pipeline to the mayors, and American cities have more democratic political processes with racial and ethnic participation, Professor Byrne said.[82] For example, Professor Byrne related, in the *Kelo* case, the New London City Council went through an elaborate political process—a discussion—before it approved the use of eminent domain under the state-funded redevelopment program.[83] Professor Byrne said Justice Stevens described the project as an appropriate remedy for [*economic distress that was not blight*][84] when he wrote the Supreme Court's opinion. Professor Byrne concluded that we have come a long way, but can do more to make participation better.[85]

Mr. Shelton agreed with Professor Somin that those without political or economic power still face many challenges from the use of eminent domain. Because the African American community is disproportionately poor and their property values are correspondingly low, their homes are an attractive bargain to developers seeking to buy many lots for a major project.[86] Many residents feel that they have not had an opportunity to participate in decisions to locate the projects in their neighborhoods, and the NAACP recommends addressing these concerns. At the same time, Mr. Shelton agreed with Commissioner Yaki that a number of eminent domain projects have helped the poor living in those communities.[87] In Brooklyn and Manhattan, major construction projects allowed the displaced poor to return, receiving first priority on rent-controlled units at the same rate as they paid before. Mr. Shelton hoped to see more such examples across the country. He again lamented that major projects often create situations where the displaced people cannot afford to return to the communities they left.[88]

Commissioner Yaki agreed with Mr. Shelton and interjected that, for the Mission Bay project in San Francisco, he had negotiated setting aside a proportion of homes for low-income, permanent rentals and home ownership. The city provided affordable housing to ensure that the community was diversified and to allow the return of any displaced people, although the project displaced very few residents, Commissioner Yaki said.[89]

Mr. Shelton then added that compensation for displacement under eminent domain does not consider the value of informal "capital" arrangements found in low- and moderate-income neighborhoods. For example, he said, one mother babysits while another shops for groceries, and brings home food items for both families. Mr. Shelton noted that compensation for displacement must consider the value of such arrangements.[90]

Finally, in contrast to Professor Byrne's and Mr. Shelton's responses to Commissioner Yaki's question, Professor Beito did not agree that instances of eminent domain abuse were rare today, citing his previously described examples in Montgomery, Alabama.[91]

Vice Chair Thernstrom said she knew about eminent domain from her 10 years served on the board of the Institute for Justice, which brought national public attention to *Kelo* and related issues. She disputed Professor Byrne's description of eminent domain decisions as local democracy at work, reflecting the political judgment of the local communities, particularly in New London, Connecticut, where local government took unblighted homes of lower middle-class people.[92] While Professor Byrne attributed the public reaction in the New London case to the fact that middle-class whites owned the displaced homes,[93] Vice Chair Thernstrom suggested that the outcry arose because the processes of eminent domain were insufficiently democratic and needed more publicity.[94]

In response, Professor Somin explained why he believed the residents' political participation was insufficient to protect their rights. At some level, he said, one can characterize almost any local government action as democracy. Nonetheless, many exercises of local democracy may have the support of the majority of the population and still violate the Constitution. He cited censorship, racial discrimination, and unreasonable searches and seizures as examples. Professor Somin thereby justified the need for constitutional rights to constrain local government.[95]

Furthermore, Professor Somin said, voters and residents often had little influence on takings in New London and elsewhere. First, many projects are complex and difficult for non-experts to learn what is going on or to knowledgably assess them, particularly when the economic development that purportedly justifies the taking may not be evident until years later.[96] Second, politically-connected developers and powerful interest groups are involved in the process. In the New London case, the Pfizer Corporation lobbied for the taking. At that time, the chair of the New London Development Corporation, the quasi-governmental agency that organized the condemnation, was the spouse of a Pfizer executive.[97] Professor Somin believes that the chair undertook the condemnation because she believed it was in the public interest, not just because it would benefit Pfizer. But, Professor Somin said, such connections influence perceptions of what is in the public interest. So an exercise of local democracy may work poorly and is often heavily influenced by interest groups, Professor Somin said, further arguing for constitutional rights that constrain local government.[98]

Professor Somin agreed with the panel that the increase in African Americans' political power in urban areas was progress, but still feared abuse because eminent domain takings target the urban and minority poor who have very limited political influence. Indeed, to stay in office, politicians favor the interest of those with political leverage over those who lack it, he said.[99]

Professor Byrne, having belatedly agreed that the *Kelo* case did not apply a blight finding, said that local officials proceeded under what they believed was a more transparent procedure provided in Connecticut state law. This provision allowed eminent domain use in response to a finding of economic distress if local authorities could show that the project would address the city's problem.[100] Professor Byrne further explained that Connecticut officials were trying to avoid the broad and troublesome definition of "blight" that federal law uses to declare a need for economic development.[101]

Professor Byrne said that members of the Connecticut Supreme Court concluded that the New London Development Corporation and the City Council that approved the project did not redevelop the area to benefit Pfizer, but because the planners hoped the presence of the Pfizer test facility would attract other corporate development. According to Professor Byrne, favoritism did not factor into the decision.[102] Professor Byrne concluded that politics at both the local and federal levels are subject to powerful entities' influence, but the remedies are more transparency and local participation in the decision process, not taking away local governments' powers to engage in economic redevelopment.[103]

Chairman Castro expressed concern about a new Pew Research Center report showing that the net worth of minorities, especially Latinos and African Americans, plummeted to far less than that of white Americans during recent economic conditions. While homes comprise most of minorities' accumulated wealth, Chairman Castro said, he asked Professor Byrne if entrepreneurial efforts were also a source of success,[104] and whether eminent domain requirements should or do provide compensation for displaced businesses and distinguish between family-owned or -run businesses and corporate entities. Professor Byrne responded that he supported providing displacement compensation for viable small businesses, as Mr. Shelton had suggested.[105] Professor Byrne said he feared that any proposal to prohibit the use of eminent domain for economic development would also prevent the acquisition of vacant lots that investors own for speculation, where no "going concern," i.e., viable business, exists. He noted that remedies that increase compensation for eminent domain displacement merit further study.[106]

Commissioner Gaziano asked Professors Byrne and Somin to react to two assumptions. First, he questioned Professor Byrne's implication that libertarians were concerned only about the scope of government power and not the plight of minorities and the poor.[107] Second, Commissioner Gaziano doubted Professor Byrne's suggestion that, when government has the right motives, it will usually help minorities more. Racism may no longer drive eminent domain use, Commissioner Gaziano said, but history reveals many mistakes in urban renewal programs, citing the huge housing projects in which the U.S. Department of Housing and Urban Development segregated minorities decades ago. Commissioner Gaziano inquired as to whether one should trust the government, even when its intentions are wellmeaning.[108]

Professor Byrne stated that libertarians could sincerely care about victims of racial discrimination.[109] Nonetheless, in his view, the Institute for Justice, Professor Somin, and Commissioner Gaziano side with property owners in an endeavor to eliminate eminent domain use for economic development, instead of focusing on the undue impact of eminent domain on minorities, the topic of the Commission's briefing.[110] Professor Byrne said that eliminating eminent domain for economic development does not address the harm to minorities that traditional projects, such as highways or public housing, cause. Constraining its use also takes away cities' tool to maintain economic competitiveness through the development of greenfield sites. Furthermore, he said, Commissioner Gaziano and others, such as the late Bernard Siegan, argue against government regulating land use.[111] Because of some recent and past government mistakes in policy on urban development, urban renewal has had mixed success. However, Professor Byrne argued that urban planning has improved since the 1950s. "We have ... less grandiose ideas" and better "understand the value of mixed development" and "the limited role that government can play" in redeveloping areas. Whether government has a role in planning and regulating land use is a broader question than the issue of eminent domain, he asserted. Nonetheless, some uses of eminent domain in the last decade were very beneficial, Professor Byrne said, because government can overcome holdouts and assemble plots of land, unlike private developers, and can insist on involving the community in the planning process, which is "valuable."[112]

Acknowledging that he was a libertarian, Professor Somin said he advocated for the same property rights for the poor and the wealthy alike, just as the constitutional right to freedom of speech protects both large businesses and individuals with unpopular opinions.[113] Yet, poor and politically-weak property owners are more vulnerable to abuse of their rights, he said, and the government should protect them. Professor Somin explained that he became libertarian in part because he perceived that the government favored the politically powerful over the weak, particularly when the general public cannot easily scrutinize complex issues, such as eminent domain.[114] Professor Somin noted that the government's problems are systemic and do not stem from particular planning processes or individuals making redevelopment decisions.[115] At the same time, in his view, urban planners overstate the proper government role. He suggested that private developers can overcome problems such as holdouts without resorting to eminent domain, possibly through secret assembly. Furthermore, when developers fund projects through their own sources, rather than with government monies, they have greater incentives to develop projects that promote rather than destroy economic growth.[116] For example, the government spent $80 million in public funds in the *Kelo* project, yet today the property lies empty at a significant economic loss, years after the taking. In many instances, developers with public funds have built structures that produce less economic development than if they had only private monies for the projects.[117]

Professor Somin agreed that similar problems may arise with traditional takings for roads and the like, and merit attention; however, he believes that such takings are better justified than condemnations that transfer land to private parties. He added that he supports having public scrutiny of any large publicly-funded assembly project, not the secret operations private developers often employ.[118]

Commissioner Heriot asked Professor Somin what is more effective in overcoming urban blight than the use of eminent domain.[119] Professor Somin recommended addressing blight, that is, dilapidated areas with threats to public health, through: (1) sustaining long-term economic growth, (2) protecting property rights, (3) imposing public health codes in areas breeding infectious diseases, (4) bringing nuisance abatement and private lawsuits to target specific concerns, and (5) promoting legislation for more private planned communities where people purchase their homes and voluntarily cooperate in community improvements.[120] He added that people are often more interested in participating in improving the planned communities in which they live than in political processes concerning the use of eminent domain.[121] Professor Somin implied that these approaches are advantageous because they do not forcibly displace people from their homes or businesses. He added parenthetically that takings targeting small businesses often inflict as much harm as those that target homes, even though those cases draw less public sympathy.[122]

Commissioner Kladney asked Professor Somin about his assessment of redevelopment using eminent domain in New York City's Times Square and in Las Vegas, Nevada. Commissioner Kladney believed that a redevelopment plan was successful in removing the blight in Times Square during the early

1980s.[123] Professor Somin clarified that he objected to the use of eminent domain in Times Square in the mid-1990s (that led to a 2001 court decision, nearly two decades after the timeframe to which Commissioner Kladney referred), because the taking transferred property that was not blighted to the *New York Times* to build a new headquarters.[124] In downtown Las Vegas—the *Pappas* case[125]— Professor Somin objected to the use of eminent domain because of the state's broad definition of blight. The land owners claimed the area was not blighted; but Nevada's definition of blight then included any area less developed than the potential of an alternative use. The Nevada Supreme Court ruled that the property was blighted based on this definition.[126]

Commissioner Kladney next asked if any case had shown a violation of civil rights or property rights or whether *Kelo* or the *Hawaiian Housing Authority*[127] had withstood any courts' tests for constitutionality.[128] Professor Somin replied that *Kelo* was a close Supreme Court decision (4-5) and that he and many others believe that the majority's opinion was wrong. Some lower court decisions have struck down takings on the basis that the official rationale was pretextual and a number of state Supreme Court decisions invalidated *Kelo*-like takings under their state constitutions, he said. [129] In part because the government has won most of the cases, especially those in federal court, in Professor Somin's view, the cases indicate that the federal and some state courts have not sufficiently protected property rights.[130]

Commissioner Yaki commented that he wished the Commission could use its subpoena power to further explore the method Professor Beito described that officials used in Montgomery to take and demolish homes that mostly African Americans owned. Commissioner Yaki then asked Professor Somin about the democracy of alternatives to eminent domain for amassing large plots of land, such as secret assembly, where developers buy small parcels hoping to unite them.[131] His observations of cities throughout the country suggest that developers pay no more than the government would for some properties, certainly not the highest investment price; and they use shell corporations to undemocratically obscure the fact that only one entity is making many purchases.[132]

Commissioner Yaki said that secret assembly methods do not address community concerns such as where the displaced residents will go; whether they will receive relocation assistance, special privileges or incentives to return; what type of development will occur; and whether the project is a good and efficient use of property. With secret assembly, these questions are not addressed until developers approach the planning commission to begin construction when the opportunities to involve the community or reduce the impact on minorities are limited.[133]

Commissioner Yaki asked whether the undemocratic aspects of alternative methods such as secret assembly mitigate against the ills Professor Somin perceives in the use of eminent domain.[134] Professor Somin responded that with any voluntary assembly, whether secret or not, property owners need not sell unless they agree to the payment offered and feel better off with the money than the property, whether or not it is the highest or best price. With property rights, owners can refuse an offer if they feel they will be worse off living elsewhere. That is a fundamental difference from eminent domain, he said.[135] Furthermore, Professor Somin conceded that community members could not participate in planning a secret project until it became public. Although this may seem undemocratic, he said, they have more influence in the disposition of their property through accepting or refusing buyers' offers than through the small voice they might have in the political process for using eminent domain.

Professor Somin believed that residents choosing to sell or retain their properties was fairer and would maximize economic efficiency and economic development more than the use of eminent domain.[136] He explained that, when the current owners of the property value their land more than the developer does, then secret assembly achieves better economic growth or efficiency than eminent domain, because it sifts out projects that are worth less than the existing uses that they would displace.[137]

Commissioner Achtenberg asked Professor Byrne whether recent data and statistics on eminent domain use are sufficient for alleging that it disparately affects minorities and other disempowered communities.[138] Professor Byrne agreed with Commissioner Achtenberg that policymakers lack empirical studies meeting rigorous social science standards that examine the recent use of eminent domain or determine its incidence and who it affects.[139] He criticized a study[140] of "victims" of eminent domain abuse that merely examines the population characteristics of the Census tracts in which eminent domain was used. That, he said, "doesn't tell ... very much." Across the political spectrum, all agree that we need research to gain a better understanding of what occurs.[141]

COMMISSIONERS' STATEMENTS AND REBUTTALS

Statement of Chairman Martin R. Castro with Commissioner Roberta Achtenberg Concurring

> "Property is intended to serve life, and no matter how much we surround it with rights and respect, it has no personal being. It is part of the earth man walks on. It is not man."
>
> --Martin Luther King, Jr.

I was pleased to vote in favor of the Commission conducting this briefing on the potential civil rights implications of the use of the eminent domain power, for several reasons: (1) there was bipartisan interest in the topic both inside and outside of the Commission, and we can always use more bipartisanship—especially at the Commission; (2) if indeed there was a widespread, current pattern of abuse of the eminent domain power based on race and ethnicity, then this Commission should be looking into the issue; and (3) it allowed us to examine an issue at the national level that was initially raised by one of our State Advisory Committees as I am a firm believer in the concept that our work at the Commission, at least in part, should be informed by the work taking place within our State Advisory Committees.

However, after reviewing the materials prepared for our briefing, reading the written submissions of our witnesses, and hearing their testimony at our briefing, I am not convinced that there is currently a widespread or systemic abuse of the eminent domain power that is having a disparate impact on communities of color, or is being directed at racial and ethnic minority communities in a discriminatory fashion. What I am certain of is that there are isolated abuses, which the witnesses and the materials highlighted for us, and those should be of concern and the circumstances that lead to them should be corrected. However, the greatest abuses presented to the Commission as part of our briefing were, for the most part, abuses, which took place decades ago.

In recent years there has been a massive loss of property among people of color, especially among Latinos and African-Americans. That loss is of minorities' homes as a result of the mortgage foreclosure crisis. This issue, more than the current use of eminent domain, has deprived the most vulnerable in our society of their property, and for many, their sole asset—their homes. It is this issue, and not eminent domain use (or alleged abuse), that has plunged African-Americans and Latinos into greater depths of poverty and decimated what little wealth they had managed to build, especially compared to their White neighbors.[1] This Commission should seriously examine the disparate impact of this issue on minority communities.

What I found fascinating about this briefing is how my conservative colleagues suddenly embraced the concept of "disparate impact" on minority communities when it comes to eminent domain, while rejecting the notion of disparate impact when it comes to our recent briefings on disparate treatment of minority students in school discipline, or in the disparate impact of the use of criminal background checks in employment. It reminds me of something my mom used to say about people who would change what they said depending on the circumstances: "lo hacen cuando les conviene," which translates to "they do it when it suits their needs." In the instant case I agree with Prof. Byrne that conservatives, especially Libertarians, are using minorities as a foil to advance their concern regarding their view of government intrusion on property rights in economic development projects. Truth be told, as was pointed out in our briefing, much more harm has been done to minority property rights and minority communities over the decades as the result of the taking of property by governments for highways and other "purely public" uses, yet that was not the focus of this issue brought to the Commission.

I also agree with Prof. Byrne that economic revitalization projects actually benefit minority communities rather than harm them because they create jobs and increase tax revenues which those disproportionately minority communities can in turn utilize for such important items such as education and increased services. I would add to this list the reduction of violence flowing to communities of color where economic revitalization is catalyzed.

It would have also been useful for our Commission to hear from local government officials as well as residents affected by the use of eminent domain.

One thing I think we can all agree upon is that there is a true lack of empirical data on the impact of eminent domain use on communities of color. I regret that our Commission no longer has the resources as we did in our early history to conduct such original research. Therefore, I hope someone with the resources can conduct such impartial and empirical research and perhaps then this Commission can address this issue if indeed communities of color are actually harmed by the current use of eminent domain in our localities.

While the Commission as a whole did not make any recommendations as a result of this briefing, as Chairman, I would urge those policy-makers who review this report to act on the following recommendations made by some of our panelists, which I adopt as part of my Statement:

Chairman's Recommendations

(1) Providing more procedural protections or compensation to residents than to commercial property owners;

(2) Mandating minimum payments to tenants, who now receive no compensation when rental housing is condemned and they are forced to move;

(3) Amending the Fair Housing Act to clarify that it applies to condemnation of residences without regard to intent;

(4) Be open and transparent and guarantee the full participation of any affected communities;

(5) Provide fair compensation covering replacement costs for the takings, not just the appraisal value, so that those displaced are not worse off; and

(6) That there be an unbiased, empirical study using rigorous social science standards, examining the current impact on communities of color of the use of the eminent domain power by local governments.

(7) The U.S. Department of Justice's Civil Rights Division should establish a task force to examine the application and subsequent implications of eminent domain laws across the country. The task force should focus on creating a standard formula used to determine just compensation, taking into consideration the implications of eminent domain on migration patterns and the economic impact of eminent domain use on the re-developed areas. The task force should consider the feasibility of alternatives such as, but not limited to (1) providing more procedural protections or compensation to residents than commercial property owners, (2) mandating minimum payments to tenants who now receive no compensation when rental housing is condemned and they are forced to move, and (3) amending the Fair Housing Act to clarify that it applies to condemnation of residences without regard to intent.

The Civil Rights Implications of Eminent Domain Abuse Statement of Vice Chair Abigail Thernstrom

Is the use or abuse of eminent domain a proper subject for the U.S. Commission on Civil Rights to address?

A traditional view of civil rights addresses abridgments of one's rights based on color, race, religion, sex, age, disability, or national origin, or in the administration of justice.

But, as one panelist succinctly put it:

> [P]roperty and the ownership of it were actually at the heart of the conception of civil rights that underlay the enactment of the Fourteenth Amendment. It was central to the rights that the framers of that amendment hoped to guarantee to African Americans and to other minorities.[1]

Yet, with considerable justification, some scholars refer to property rights as the poor step child of civil rights because they are so easily abridged, even violated, often seemingly arbitrarily, by our own government.

Using eminent domain to seize private property from one owner and transfer it to another for "economic development" is fundamentally different from, and more constitutionally suspect than, declaring eminent domain for a truly "public use" such as building roads, schools, or other infrastructure. The very definition of "public use" has become ambiguous and controversial.

As was discussed at our briefing, it is a fact that often in our past eminent domain has been deliberately used in a racially discriminatory manner. However, in our more recent past that dynamic has shifted. Today eminent domain is not motivated by racial animus but by the profit motive or, as some would describe it, greed. As it happens, the property owners most likely to fail in fighting off eminent domain—and against whom wealthy developers are most likely to prevail—are the politically and economically powerless, a large proportion of whom happen to be minorities. To argue today that eminent domain is racially discriminatory is to invite a debate about disparate impact.

Our report describes one perspective on disparate impact and eminent domain:

> Commissioner Achtenberg asked Professor Byrne whether recent data and statistics on eminent domain use are sufficient for alleging that it disparately affects minorities and other disempowered communities. Professor Byrne agreed with Commissioner Achtenberg that policy makers lack empirical studies meeting rigorous social science standards that examine the recent use of eminent domain or determine its incidence and who it affects. He criticized a study of "victims" of eminent domain abuse that merely examines the population characteristics of the Census tracts in which eminent domain was used. That, he said, "doesn't tell ... very much." Across

the political spectrum, all agree that we need research to gain a better understanding of what occurs.[2]

I have long held that mere disparity in the effect of an otherwise non-discriminatory action does not constitute proof of illegal racial discrimination.

A very relevant case involving *both* eminent domain *and* disparate impact is currently pending before the U.S. Supreme Court. The case is *Mount Holly v. Mt. Holly Gardens Citizens in Action*[3]. It involves a redevelopment plan to convert a blighted Mount Holly neighborhood into more upscale (more expensive), single family homes. The residents opposing this plan are mostly non-white and have raised a disparate impact claim against the condemnation.

The case hinges on whether disparate impact claims are cognizable under the Fair Housing Act (FHA). A central legal issue is that the FHA does not contain language providing for liability based on nondiscriminatory actions. This Supreme Court would likely rule that FHA does not allow such claims. As happened in a similar, previous case intense political pressure has been brought to bear to reach a settlement and keep *Mt. Holly* from being heard by the Supreme Court.[4] As this statement is being written the parties may already have approved a settlement and the high court won't have the opportunity to address this important question during this term.[5]

Conclusion

Property rights and the protection of those rights represent one of our most basic civil rights and should be treated as such. The protection of property rights should be enforced at least as vigorously as other civil rights such as the right not to be discriminated against because of one's race or gender.

Also, as we were informed at our briefing, the "just compensation" given to property owners whose land has been seized seldom fully compensates the owners for less tangible but important things such as convenience of location, neighborhood networks and relationships, conveniently located parks and other facilities, convenience to transit, and other factors.

Finally, "public use" needs to be defined more narrowly and needs to be weighted in favor of the property owners whose land has been condemned, not the other way around. Private-to-private property transfers via eminent domain should be rare rather than common, and the purported economic benefits of redevelopment condemnations must be rigorously defined prior to the transaction. Subsequently, if the economic benefits fail to materialize, there should be consequences which should be formulated in such a way as to discourage use of eminent domain for speculative redevelopment schemes.

U.S. Commission on Civil Rights Statement for "The Civil Rights Implications of Eminent Domain Abuse" Commissioner Roberta Achtenberg

November 9, 2013

Examining government's exercise of the Takings Clause of the Fifth Amendment to the United States Constitution is neither simple nor without controversy. The Report and the Commission's full record in this matter raise two issues of particular concern. Both the lack of recent data and the definition of the "just compensation" due in exchange for government's exercise of eminent domain powers merit comment.

I. Lack of Data

The Commission's record does not contain information from recent decades about the incidence and seriousness of disparate impact of eminent domain takings upon the classes of people within the Commission's jurisdiction.[1]

I agree with Commissioner Kladney, as he writes in his individual Statement, that the Commission has "not seen a satisfactory case presented that present-day uses of eminent domain amount to discrimination or denial of equal protection on the basis of race or ethnicity [citing 42 USC 1975a(a)]."[2]

I questioned both the lack of the most pertinent types of data and the absence of recent data during the August 12, 2011 briefing.[3]

The federal government should ensure the development of current statistics regarding the exercise of Fifth Amendment eminent domain powers and what, if any impact (disparate or otherwise) there has been on racial and ethnic minority communities. The government should achieve this goal by funding research into the scope and impact of recent exercises of eminent domain power through HUD, other government agencies, and/or grants to colleges, universities and private research firms. The government should fund research examining at least the years from 2000 through the present so that any impact of the recent economic recession and recovery efforts upon the takings issue can be investigated.

New research should document, at a minimum, the number and types of takings, the governmental entities exercising eminent domain power, the "public use" justifications given, and the discernible impact upon displaced low-income minority residential and commercial property owners, tenants, and other involved communities.

New research addressing the impact of takings upon those who appear to be at elevated risk of displacement could be especially valuable in addressing my second area of concern: that of just compensation. Research that fosters understanding of the scope of the problems faced by racial and ethnic minorities may help underscore the need for a more comprehensive set of remedies.

II. Just Compensation

Residential and commercial tenants do not always receive just compensation for their leasehold interests in properties which are taken by eminent domain powers.[4] This reality ignores the economic and intangible values of businesses and of informal social support networks within low-income minority communities which ease and enhance residents' quality of life, such as cooperative child care and food shopping.[5] When takings occur, just compensation should be granted to residential and commercial tenants as well as to property owners.

The calculation of just compensation for both owners and tenants should take into account business losses and replacement costs, increased post-displacement rental rates, and the intangible harm done to communities of relocated low-income minority residents. Just compensation should be expanded to include both monetary and non-monetary (or in-kind) compensation to tenants who, under a strict "fair market" valuation of just compensation, may currently receive nothing.

A key element in mitigating the harm that displaced communities suffer is the immediate provision of affordable, safe housing. Takings-related affordable housing practice should become comprehensive. Members of displaced communities could well benefit from guaranteed transfer to public housing units created within the redeveloped areas, interim public housing or Section 8 certificates if necessary until the provision of such housing, payment for moving expenses, and other quality-of-life elements.

Statement and Rebuttal of Commissioner Gail Heriot

My colleague Commissioner Kirsanow proposed this briefing to highlight the disparate impact of eminent domain takings on racial and ethnic minorities.

I was pleased with the resulting briefing and with this report, which provides useful additional information on the causes of this disproportionate effect and potential responses to the aggressive use of the eminent domain power.

Like many of my conservative colleagues on the Commission, I am often skeptical of proposals to cast some social ill as a discrimination issue simply because of its disproportionate effect on some racial or ethnic group. Some of my colleagues suggest that being concerned about the adverse effects of eminent domain is in tension with positions that my conservative colleagues and I have taken elsewhere on laws that heavily restrict employment or educational practices that have a disparate impact on some protected group. See Draft Statement of Chairman Castro at 2;[1] Draft Statement of Commissioner Kladney at 3. It is one thing to suggest that a racially adverse effect merits greater public attention than it has so far received. It is quite a leap to move from that observation to the conclusion that Congress must pass laws sharply limiting the use of eminent domain solely because of that racial effect. Just so that the point is crystal clear, I am not in favor of any such federal law.

The proper exercise of governments' eminent domain power is a complicated question, and getting the right answer requires considering many questions besides its racially adverse effects. Among them: What does the Fifth Amendment to the United States Constitution permit?[2] Do "hold-outs" who decline to sell their land to private developers present a threat to the success of beneficial, large-scale development projects such that the exercise of eminent domain is appropriate? What are the benefits to the broad community and what are the costs of such takings? Are there alternative ways of achieving those benefits?[3] Many of these questions lie outside the Commission's traditional purview or my own expertise, and I've therefore tried to strike a modest tone in this statement.

I nonetheless found this briefing topic worthy of study because eminent domain's racially adverse effect seems counterintuitive to many people.[4] Conventional wisdom has it that robust judicial protections of property rights redound only to the benefit of wealthy and privileged groups, and that ever-morepowerful government will always be the friend of the poor and historically discriminated against.[5] The story told in this briefing report counsels otherwise.

In the nineteenth century, protecting the property rights of freed slaves was seen as a crucial means of securing meaningful freedom for them. Professor David Beito's testimony quoted Frederick Douglass on the subject: "We hold the civil government to be solemnly bound to protect the weak against the strong, the oppressed against the oppressor, the few against the many, and to secure *the humblest subject in the full possession of his rights of person and of property*."[6] (Italics added.) The framers of the Fourteenth Amendment took similar views. They worried that Southern state and local governments would threaten the property rights of freed slaves and those whites who supported the Union and therefore understood private property to be one of the core rights to be protected by the Amendment.[7]

Widespread use of eminent domain did not appear as a major challenge to traditional conceptions of property rights for another several decades, when early twentieth century progressives became interested in strategies for improving American cities. To put the point gently, most did not share the racial sensibilities and multiculturalist ideals of twenty-first century progressives. Instead, these advocates sought to make cities more "rational" by displacing members of undesirable racial and ethnic groups who they believed impeded "hygienic" or "scientific" urban development. The term "blight," which Progressive intellectuals borrowed from botany, in effect likened the spread of such people to invasive plant diseases.[8] The 1954 landmark *Berman v. Parker* decision, which authorized a broad conception of "public use," reflected decades of sustained efforts by these advocates to reshape the jurisprudence of eminent domain to achieve their goals more easily.[9] The neighborhood of southwest Washington, D.C., in which the *Berman* condemnations took place was also overwhelmingly African-American.[10]

Advocates for the prominent redevelopment projects of mid-century were often quite up front about their intentions to use urban renewal projects for racially discriminatory ends. As quoted in the body of this report, displacement of African-Americans and urban renewal projects were so intertwined that urban renewal was referred to as "Negro removal."[11] In Chicago in the 1940s, protesters claimed that the "Lake Meadows" re-development project on the near Southside was "Negro clearance" rather than "slum clearance" and said, "If it is a slum clearance program, then let's make it that and start where the slums are." Although their complaints delayed the project, these efforts ultimately did not stop the clearance of the area.[12] In New York, a leading proponent of the 1940s "Stuyvesant Town" redevelopment project, Metropolitan Life Insurance Chairman Frederick Ecker, infamously defended the company's decision to deny admission to blacks by declaring that "blacks and whites just don't mix."[13] One study reports that, between 1949 and 1973, government officials executed 2,532 projects in 992 cities, displacing one million people, two-thirds of whom were African American.[14]

Eminent domain use displaced African Americans five times more often than their representation in the nation's population.[15]

Fortunately, aggressively racial motivations for takings appear less common now than they were a few decades ago. But it remains at best unclear whether redevelopment advocates have fully acknowledged or grappled with some of the more unsavory facets of the intellectual history of "blight" and of *Berman v. Parker*, which remain integral parts of contemporary takings law. Indeed, the latter was re-affirmed in, and largely drove the outcome of, the more recent *Kelo v. New London.*[16]

The best evidence available to the Commission also indicates that eminent domain takings still disproportionately affect minority neighborhoods.[17] The accounts of eminent domain use in Birmingham collected by David Beito and discussed in a forthcoming Alabama SAC report further suggest cause for concern. This appears to be so for several reasons. First, racial and ethnic minorities are vulnerable because their properties tend to be less valuable. Condemning authorities can pay less compensation for taking them and realize greater profits if the properties appreciate in value. Second, minority residents sometimes lack the political influence necessary to block takings, at least in part because of past discrimination. They also are less likely to be in a position to challenge takings in court.[18]

Home ownership presents an important opportunity for poor and minority families to integrate into the middle class.[19] Stable property rights encourage home ownership. Conversely, the Commission heard testimony that the threat of takings in disproportionately poor and minority communities can lead to declines in property values and discourage families from investing there.[20]

A displaced family may not just lose its home. Family members may also lose the community at their church, their daughter's Girl Scout Troop, or the arrangement whereby one mother of young children babysits two children while the other buys groceries for both families—what the sociology textbooks sometimes dryly call "social capital" generated by "civil society." All of us value and can benefit from such institutions. But poor families with fewer resources—who might struggle to otherwise afford babysitting or who would particularly appreciate a "hand up" from a local church—may value them especially. Genuine as the value of such social capital is, it is also difficult to assess and to provide families with money as "just compensation" for it. Further, history is replete with examples of how thriving civil society institutions have helped disadvantaged groups integrate into the wider society and how they have served as bulwarks against ever-growing government.[21] Only a fool would believe the vast network of civil relationships—from having Aunt Suzie live next door to singing in the choir of the Bethel Memorial A.M.E. Church to being a member of the local V.F.W. Post—can be replaced with a new federal program of the U.S. Department of Health and Human Services.

I acknowledge, as witness Hilary Shelton testified, that "traditional" uses of eminent domain will also often have a disparate impact on minority groups. As he proposed, procedural safeguards[22] and adequate compensation may help offset some of those takings' harms. But the traditional conception of public use tends to be self-limiting. The demand for additional roads or schools tends to be limited. Politicians often hesitate to fund the construction of costly new public works projects unless there appears to be genuine public demand for them. And at least such projects can be potentially used by all of the public and not just by a private developer or one private firm. On the other hand, the broad *Kelo* formulation of public use permitting economic development takings will likely lead to many more takings. *Kelo* requires only that the taking is likely to contribute to economic growth (and it requires courts to largely accept the government's assertions of such growth essentially at face value). But virtually any commercial enterprise will contribute to economic growth to some degree (however small), meaning that this limitation is really not much limit at all. Indeed, the number of takings for private economic development appears to have gone up in the wake of *Kelo*.[23] As Justice O'Connor put it in dissent in *Kelo*, "Nothing is to prevent the State from replacing any Motel 6 with a Ritz-Carlton, any home with a shopping mall, or any farm with a factory." *Kelo* at 503.[24] Or, as counsel for New London suggested in a response to a question at oral argument, it is permissible to take from A and give to B whenever B pays more in tax revenue than A.[25]

The best evidence available to the Commission suggests that these economic development projects sometimes failed to deliver the promised benefits that might offset their costs—whether to racial and ethnic minorities or anyone else. Consider the famous example of the condemnations in the Poletown neighborhood of Detroit, in which the promised plant opened two years behind schedule and at which job creation significantly lagged behind promises initially made to the city.[26] The condemnations in the *Kelo* case also have failed thus far to lead to the planned redevelopment. Instead, a group of feral cats occupying Susette Kelo's old neighborhood appear to be the main beneficiaries of the New London takings.[27] This is perhaps not surprising. Private investors want to invest in development schemes that look likely to succeed. Conversely, they avoid investing in those that look like they will not. Developers with business plans that look to many to fall into the latter category may be more likely to use political connections to secure their objectives through condemnations. As I have suggested above, one might argue that it is worthwhile to overlook the racially adverse effects of a public policy if that policy is constitutional and has other clear benefits.[28] But it is not at all clear that eminent domain for private use generally has such beneficial effects.

Conclusion

So far as I have been able to tell, everyone with whom I have had the honor of serving on the Commission (Republican, Democrat, and independent; conservative, liberal, libertarian and progressive alike) cares genuinely about the welfare of poor Americans and about ameliorating the ill effects of decades of slavery and past race discrimination. I was disappointed to read insinuations to the contrary in some of my fellow commissioners' statements. Where we do differ, as I see it, is that some of my colleagues appear to disagree that limited government and rigorous enforcement of equal protection and property rights is the best way to achieve those common goals. Although I recognize that the proper scope of governments' eminent domain power is a complex question, one that draws on many considerations, I hope that I have been able to sketch out here how a restrained approach to eminent domain can help accomplish our shared ends.

Statement on Eminent Domain
By: Dave Kladney

November 2013

The August 12, 2011 briefing on the civil rights implications of eminent domain was my first briefing at the Commission. After reviewing the background materials and then participating in the briefing itself, I have not seen a satisfactory case presented that present-day uses of eminent domain amount to discrimination or denial of equal protection on the basis of race or ethnicity.[1] Instead, what our examination of eminent domain seems to show is that, as with many things, the wealthy are able to take advantage of the less well-off.

The scope of the U.S. Commission on Civil Rights is clear; we are primarily concerned with color, race, religion, sex, age, disability, national origin.[2] However, this briefing highlighted the fact that economic disparities in our society frequently influence our charge by affecting the aforementioned classes of Americans most severely.

The studies presented during our briefing showed that instead of using race as a determinant, "communities are somewhat more likely to pursue redevelopment in poor areas than in more affluent ones."[3] None of the evidence presented in the arguments against eminent domain suggested that localities aimed the particular takings at minority property-owners. Rather, the testimony suggests that local governments singled out these property-holders because they were poor.[4]

For example, Mr. Beito's description of the mistreatment experienced by Mr. McCall and Ms. Jones does not stem from racial discrimination or eminent domain laws, per se. In Mr. McCall's case, government officials razed his property in violation of a court order barring their actions.[5] The law and the courts did their respective parts to protect Mr. McCall. It was local officials that, according to Mr. Beito, violated Mr. McCall's property rights. Just the same, Ms. Jones' mistreatment did not stem from discrimination based on her race. Unfortunately, the city's ineffective record keeping and notification requirements resulted in the demolition of her property.[6,7]

The fact that individuals abused otherwise lawful government power to exercise eminent domain for economic development is no reason to eliminate that power. After all, every power has the potential for abuse. Instead of eliminating eminent domain, affected communities would benefit more from implementation of additional procedures that curb abuses and mistakes like the ones experienced by Mr. McCall and Ms. Jones.

Beyond miscategorizing this issue as discrimination or denial of equal protection based on race, this briefing also failed to demonstrate that eminent domain is relevant as a current civil rights issue. Despite my requests[8] during the briefing for data about recent instances of eminent domain abuse that fall within our jurisdiction, none of the witnesses pointed to cases after 1973. Only after they revised their statements for the record were any of the witnesses able to point to relevant cases after 1973.[9] Even then, the witnesses arguing against the government's ability to use eminent domain could only find two recent cases[10] of discrimination.[11] The first case they cite is *Poletown Neighborhood Council v. Detroit* (1981), where the city of Detroit cleared a neighborhood to make space for a General Motors plant. The neighborhood in question was mostly White, and the city's action—which favored the large corporation—

was proposed to save 6,000 jobs. If anything, this case further demonstrates that eminent domain issues are class-based, rather than racially motivated. The second case, *Kaur v. N.Y. State Urban Dev. Corp., 933 N.E.2d 721 (N.Y. 2010)*—about Columbia University's continuing expansion into Harlem's Manhattanville neighborhood—has more to do with the erroneous definition of blight and institutional power in communities than racial discrimination.[12] Using *Kaur v. N.Y. State Urban Dev. Corp., 933 N.E.2d 721 (N.Y. 2010)* to describe a recent case of eminent domain abuse is wrong because New York State probably has the most questionable procedures, which have later been ruled constitutional.

Some commentators ascribe to the notion that an area is blighted only if a building or area is dilapidated, dangerous, or disease ridden. For example, one of the witnesses boldly stated it was unbelievable that the downtown area of the City of Las Vegas experienced blight. This is consistent with most Americans' idea that Las Vegas only includes the world-famous "strip" of hotels and casinos. In fact, the major hotels and casinos of the strip do not reside in the City of Las Vegas, but rather outside the city's jurisdiction in Clark County.[13]

On the other hand, the downtown area of Las Vegas was first laid out when the city just was a small town in the early 1900's, and was once the commercial center of the city. This area of redevelopment, complained about at our briefing, was hindered by poor street design and unable to handle any quantity of traffic. The result was a string of non-competitive and run down hotels, seedy bars, strip joints, dark streets, and areas of personal and property crime. Many businesses left downtown Las Vegas for other locations in the county.

The disbelief that hotel areas in the City of Las Vegas could be blighted is wrong. In the late 1990s, city leaders determined that the downtown area was blighted. They began a plan to redevelop downtown Las Vegas. The city redesigned area streets. Since then, a major Internet sales company is leasing and renovating the old city hall. The company's employees have since populated the downtown area— choosing to rent or own residential units including newly built high-rise apartments. Private investment has followed. A successful outlet shopping center has been built and another shopping center is set for construction near the newly opened Mob Museum. On top of all that, a 500 million dollar performance arts center opened this year and three outdated hotel casinos have been completely remodeled. Other business, attractions, and governmental buildings have opened for business.

I would call this a successful project. The efforts of the redevelopment agency have sparked an economic renaissance in downtown Las Vegas.

Each state approaches the use of eminent domain in a manner consistent with the needs of *that state* and its citizenry. After the aforementioned project started, but before its evident success, Nevada decided in 2008 to impose stricter requirements on redevelopment districts. Subsequent to that, they repealed the mining industry's 150-year-old right to exercise eminent domain. California has repealed every redevelopment district in the state. Florida has taken similar action, eliminating the use of eminent domain except in extreme circumstances.[14] Still, other states have several different standards and degrees of allowing the use of eminent domain, blight, and redevelopment.

Nothing stops legislatures from modifying, changing, or repealing their laws defining blight or the use of eminent domain so long as the law meets the constraints of the Constitution. Further, citizens of some states have successfully lobbied for change in their state's eminent domain policy. Citizen-led efforts to shape eminent domain policies in the states may be the best solution to the concerns about the effects of these policies.

No one can deny the long and troubled history of eminent domain policies in America. However, the recent libertarian concern for minorities and the poor is driven more by their desire to protect their own property than any real concern about the rights of potentially disaffected communities. Couching critiques of present-day eminent domain policies in terms of harms to racial and ethnic minorities seems merely strategic, if not cynical.

My conservative colleagues are calling for a national standard on eminent domain. This seems incongruous with their call on every other subject for "laboratories of democracy." The states can, and do, pass laws for the implementation of eminent domain. These laws vary from state to state and fit the unique situations of different jurisdictions; however, they must always comply with the Fifth Amendment to the Constitution.

If the libertarians at the Institute of Justice and my conservative colleagues on the Commission are truly concerned about the pernicious effects of economic disparities, I am pleased to hear that. I believe that the Commission would be more effective in our charge to serve the American people if my colleagues also acknowledged these kinds of concerns as they relate to *all* of the issues facing the Commission.

PANELISTS' WRITTEN STATEMENTS

Ilya Somin, now Professor of Law, George Mason Law School

The Civil Rights Implications ofEminent Domain Abuse

Introduction

I am grateful for the opportunity to address the important issue of the impact of eminent domain on racial and ethnic minorities. I would like to thank Chairman Castro, Vice Chair Thernstrom, and the other commissioners for their interest in this vital question.

As President Barack Obama aptly put it, "[o]ur Constitution places the ownership of private property at the very heart of our system of liberty."[1] The protection of property rights was one of the main purposes for which the Constitution was originally adopted.[2] Unfortunately, the Supreme Court has often relegated property rights to second class status, giving them far less protection than that accorded to other constitutional rights.[3] And state and local governments have often violated those rights when it seemed politically advantageous to do so.

Americans of all racial and ethnic backgrounds have suffered from government violations of constitutional property rights. But minority groups have often been disproportionately victimized, sometimes out of racial prejudice and at other times because of their relative political weakness. Minorities are especially likely to be victimized by private to private condemnations that test the limits of the Public Use Clause of the Fifth Amendment, which requires that property can only be condemned for a "public use." These include takings allegedly justified by the need to alleviate "blight" and promote "economic development."

Part I of my testimony briefly surveys the constitutional law of eminent domain and public use. It documents the extent to which the Supreme Court has given condemning authorities a near-blank check to take property for whatever purposes they want.

Part II examines the impact of blight and economic development condemnations on minority groups. Both types of takings often victimize racial and ethnic minorities. Although such condemnations are defended on the grounds that they are needed to promote economic growth in poor communities, they often destroy far more wealth than they create. Economic development can be better promoted by other, less destructive means. African

Americans and Hispanics are targeted more often than other groups in large part because of their relative political weakness and comparatively high poverty rates. While, certainly, not all members of these groups are poor or politically weak, a disproportionately large number are.

Finally, in Part III I explain why the problem of abusive takings persists despite the wave of state reform laws adopted in response to the Supreme Court's unpopular decision upholding economic development takings in *Kelo v. City of New London*.[4] Many of the new laws actually impose little or no constraint on economic development takings. Even those that do impose meaningful restrictions usually still allow private-to-private condemnations in the types of "blighted" areas where many poor minorities live. Although post-*Kelo* reforms are a step in the right direction, much remains to be done before the property rights of poor minorities are anywhere close to fully protected.

I. The Constitutional Law of Public Use

The Fifth Amendment requires that property can only be condemned for a "public use."[5] Traditional public uses include those where the condemned land is actually "used" by the public, either by building a government-owned structure on it (such as a road or a bridge), or by constructing a privately owned facility that the owner is legally required to allow the general public to use, such as a public utility.

In *Kelo v. City of New London*, the Supreme Court ruled that the condemnation of private property for transfer to another private party in order to promote "economic development" was a permissible "public use"; indeed, it ruled that virtually any potential benefit to the public benefit or "public purpose" counts as a "public use."[6] The Court upheld the condemnation of land in New London for transfer to a private party despite the fact that the condemned property would not be owned by the government, the general public would have no right of access to it, and there was no legal requirement that the new private owners actually produce the promised "economic development" that supposedly justified the takings in the first place.

Kelo was largely consistent with two previous Supreme Court decisions that defined "public use" very broadly.[7] In the 1954 case of *Berman v. Parker*, the Court upheld the condemnation of "blighted" property for transfer to private developers and concluded that the legislature has "well-nigh conclusive" power to define public use as it sees fit.[8] *Berman's* highly permissive approach was reaffirmed in *Hawaii Housing Authority v. Midkiff* in 1984.[9]

Whatever its basis in precedent, *Kelo* was at odds with the text and original meaning of the Fifth Amendment, which do not conflate "public use" with potential "public benefit," instead limiting "public use" to cases of actual government ownership of condemned property or at least a legal right of access by the public (as in the case of public utilities).[10] *Kelo* also placed undue faith in the willingness of government officials to protect the constitutional property rights of the poor and politically weak. As historian and law professor James W. Ely, Jr. has written, "among all the guarantees of the Bill of Rights, only the public use limitation is singled out for heavy [judicial] deference" to the very government officials whose abuses of power it is meant to constrain.[11] There is little sense in recognizing a constitutional right for the purpose of curbing abuses of government power, and then leaving the definition of that right up to the discretion of the very officials whose power the right is supposed to restrict.

It should also be noted that the need to protect property rights against abusive state and local governments was one of the main reasons why the framers of the Fourteenth Amendment sought to apply the Bill of Rights to the states. Congressional supporters of the Amendment feared that southern state governments would threaten the property rights of African Americans and those whites who had supported the Union against the Confederacy during the Civil War.[12] This objective cannot easily be reconciled with allowing those very same state governments to determine what qualifies as a public use, thereby giving them a blank check to expropriate the property of both African Americans and white loyalists. The right to private property was a central component of the "civil rights" that the framers of the Fourteenth Amendment sought to protect.[13]

Whether or not *Kelo* and *Berman* were correctly decided, their effect has been to eviscerate most federal judicial oversight of the use of eminent domain. Even after *Kelo*, federal courts may strike down "pretextual" condemnations whose official rationale is a mere pretext "for the purpose of conferring a private benefit on a particular private party."[14] For the last several years, state and federal courts have struggled over the question of what qualifies as a "pretextual" taking.[15] But this restriction is unlikely to greatly constrain the use of eminent domain in the long run, since, under *Kelo*, a state or local government can still condemn property for virtually any "public purpose" that might potentially create some sort of benefit.[16] Courts are not even allowed to consider whether the claimed benefits will actually materialize or not.[17] Even a relatively robust pretextual takings doctrine is therefore unlikely to give property owners more than marginal protection against abusive condemnations.[18]

Some state courts have taken a more restrictive approach in interpreting the public use clauses of their state constitutions than the federal Supreme Court has in regards to the Fifth Amendment. Eleven state supreme courts currently forbid *Kelo*-like economic development takings.[19] Nonetheless, most states permit a wide range of private-to-private condemnations.[20]

Overall, there is currently very little federal judicial oversight of private-to-private condemnations. While some states have imposed more restrictive rules, the majority have not. Therefore, property rights in most of the country remain vulnerable to takings that transfer property from the politically weak to influential interest groups.

II. The Displacement of Minorities By Eminent Domain

Private to private condemnations are often used for the benefit of the politically powerful at the expense of the politically weak.[21] For most of American history, African Americans and other minority groups have fallen into the latter category. As a result, they have often been victimized by the use of eminent domain for "blight" and economic development takings.

The Historic Impact of Blight Condemnations

Beginning in the 1930s, many states adopted laws and constitutional amendments allowing the condemnation of "blighted" property for transfer to private parties in order to alleviate "slum-like" conditions.[22] Over the next fifty years, as many as several million Americans were expelled from their homes as a result of blight and urban renewal condemnations.[23] Numerous businesses, churches, and other community institutions were also destroyed.

The vast majority of those uprooted from their homes have been poor minorities, primarily African Americans.[24] The use of eminent domain to evict poor blacks during the post-World War II era was so common that many, including famed African American writer James Baldwin, referred to urban renewal as "Negro removal."[25] Similarly, "slum clearance" was sometimes dubbed "Negro clearance."[26] Between 1949 and 1973, some two-thirds of the over one million people displaced under takings sponsored by the Urban Renewal Act of 1949 were African American.[27] This figure understates the total impact of blight takings on blacks, because many blight condemnations were also undertaken by state and local government without federal backing.[28] Hispanic groups, such as Puerto Ricans, were also commonly targeted.[29]

In many cases, the disproportionate impact on African Americans was not merely an accidental byproduct of efforts to "clean up" bad neighborhoods. It was deliberately intended by local officials.[30] Local governments sometimes sought to rid themselves of what they called "niggertowns."[31] In most cases, those displaced by blight condemnations ended up worse off than they were before, and were not fully compensated for their losses.[32]

In 1954, the Supreme Court upheld the constitutionality of blight condemnations in *Berman v. Parker.*[33] Significantly, *Berman* upheld a blight condemnation that was part of a project that forcibly displaced over 5,000 people in a poor Washington, DC neighborhood.[34] Some 97.5 percent of them were African American.[35] Only about 300 of the 5,900 housing units constructed on the site after the takings were affordable to the former residents of the area, most of whom ended up in worse conditions elsewhere.[36] By the 1960s, the neighborhood in question was majority white.[37]

As prominent legal scholar Wendell Pritchett points out, "[t]he irony is that, at the same time it was deciding *Berman*, the Court was deciding *Brown* [*v. Board of Education*], which reflects a distrust of government (particularly local government) to protect the interests of minority groups and to treat all citizens equally."[38] Unfortunately, the Supreme Court and most other legal elites failed to grasp the contradiction between aggressive judicial oversight of school segregation on the one hand and giving local governments a blank check to use eminent domain to forcibly displace African Americans on the other. For many years, *Berman's* permissive approach to blight takings set the pattern for both state and federal judicial decisions.

Recent Developments

In more recent years, minority property rights continue to be threatened by blight and economic development takings, even though modern condemnations rarely approach the biggest ones of the 1950s in scale. The risk faced by property owners has been exacerbated by the advent of extremely broad definitions of blight that enable virtually any area to be declared blighted and condemned.

Originally, "blight" condemnations were limited to areas that fit the layperson's definition of the term: dilapidated, slum-like neighborhoods. For example, the 1938 amendment to the New York state Constitution that authorized blight condemnations was intended to limit them to "slums."[39] Over time, however, most states expanded the definition of "blight" to include virtually any area that might be considered underdeveloped in some way.[40]

State courts have ruled that even such areas as downtown Las Vegas and Times Square in New York can be declared "blighted" and condemned.[41] In two recent decisions, the New York Court of Appeals has upheld major blight condemnations based on a combination of extremely broad definitions of blight and a willingness to overlook flagrant possible bias on the part of condemning authorities in favor of powerful interest groups to which the condemned property was transferred.[42] Some states also permit pure "economic development" condemnations of the sort upheld in *Kelo v. City of New London,* where no showing of blight at all is needed.[43]

Expansive definitions of blight and pure economic development takings put a wider range of properties at risk of condemnation than before, and further imperil politically weak property owners, including minorities.[44]

Today, blight and economic development takings are not as common as in the era of large-scale urban renewal projects in the 1950s and 1960s. But they nonetheless continue to disproportionately victimize the minority poor. Recent studies show that areas populated by poor minorities are far more likely to be targeted for condemnation than other neighborhoods.[45] These patterns led the NAACP and the Southern Christian Leadership Conference to file an amicus brief urging the Supreme Court to forbid economic development takings in *Kelo*.[46] The brief emphasized that economic development takings disproportionately target the minority poor, and cited a number of recent examples.[47]

In a particularly egregious 2010 case, the New York Court of Appeals allowed the use of eminent domain to transfer a large amount of property to Columbia University in the predominantly black Manhattanville neighborhood.[48] The condemnation went through despite the fact that the firm that conducted the "blight" study that justified the condemnation had been on Columbia's payroll, and much of the blight used to justify the takings was actually on land that Columbia already owned, thereby making it likely that Columbia itself had created the "blight" that justified the use of eminent domain.[49]

As in earlier decades, blight and economic development takings often destroy far more economic value than they create, thereby actually undermining their professed goals and inflicting serious long-term harm on the communities where they occur.[50] In the *Kelo* case, for example, nothing has been built on the site of the condemned property even six years after the end of litigation, and it is not clear whether anything will be built in the foreseeable future.[51]

Prior to *Kelo,* the most famous economic development taking in American history was the 1981 *Poletown* case, in which the Michigan Supreme Court upheld a condemnation that displaced some 4,000 people in Detroit for the purpose of transferring the land to General Motors for the construction of a new factory.[52] In that case, too, the new use of the condemned property produced no more than a fraction of the promised economic growth—not enough to offset the losses caused by the destruction of numerous homes, businesses and schools, and the expenditure of some $250 million in public funds.[53]

The negative impact of eminent domain on minorities is partially offset by compensation payments. However, compensation often falls far short of fully making up for all the losses suffered by victims of eminent domain. Many studies find that property owners often do not even get the "fair market value"[54] compensation required by the Supreme Court.[55] Undercompensation is particularly likely in the case of "low value" properties of the kind often occupied by poor minority group members.[56] Even when fair market value compensation is paid, owners still are not compensated for the loss of the "subjective value" they attach to their property over and above its market valuation.[57] Subjective value includes such elements as community ties and business good will that are often lost when victims of eminent domain are forced to move their homes or businesses.

Today, the disproportionate targeting of minorities is less likely to be caused by old-fashioned racial prejudice than in the urban renewal era, and more likely to be the result of the political weakness of these groups.[58] That weakness is exacerbated by relatively high poverty rates. Some 25.8 percent of blacks and 25.3 percent of Hispanics have incomes below the poverty line, compared to 9.4 percent of whites and 12.5 percent of Asian-Americans.[59] Social science confirms the common sense view that the poor, on average, have far less political influence than more affluent citizens.[60]

Racial prejudice may still be at work in so far as public opinion is less inclined to oppose takings that harm people of different racial or ethnic groups. Ethnocentric bias influences public opinion on a variety of issues, and often affects the views of people who are not actively hostile to minorities but merely less concerned about their welfare than that of members of their own group.[61] There is a need for more research on the extent to which such "ethnocentrism" influences public opinion and policy on eminent domain. Even if present racial bias plays relatively little role in selecting targets for condemnation, past racial injustice is undeniably one of the causes of the poverty and political weakness that make blacks and some other minorities vulnerable to takings.

Minorities and the Holdout Rationale for Eminent Domain

Some scholars argue that the use of eminent domain is essential for the promotion of economic development in minority neighborhoods. They claim that it is needed to facilitate development projects that would otherwise be blocked by holdout problems.[62] If a developer needs to acquire property from many different owners in order to build his or her project, holdouts can potentially block it by refusing to sell unless they are paid a price so high as to make it unprofitable to proceed with the project.[63]

Holdouts are a genuine danger for some development projects. Fortunately, however, market participants have tools for preventing holdouts without resorting to the use of eminent domain. The most commonly used is secret assembly, under which developers purchase the property they need without revealing their purpose. This prevents potential strategic holdouts from realizing that there is a big development project that they can hold up in hopes of getting a payoff.

As a tool for preventing holdouts, secret assembly has two major advantages over eminent domain.[64] First, it incentivizes property owners to reveal their true valuation of the land they own, agreeing to sell to the would-be developer if they value the land less than he does and refusing to sell if they value it more. In this way, secret assembly helps sift out those projects that are genuinely more valuable than the preexisting uses of the property developers seek to acquire, from those that are not. If current owners value the land more than the developer does, the project will not go through, which is the correct outcome from the standpoint of economic efficiency. Even if the sole objective of public policy is to maximize economic development, it is still preferable to block projects that replace higher-value land uses with less valuable ones. By contrast, when the government uses eminent domain to acquire property, it has no way of determining whether its planned uses are more valuable than those of the current owners. Officials have no reliable means of estimating the subjective value the property has for its present users.

Second, unlike eminent domain, secret assembly cannot be "captured" by powerful interest groups for the purpose of acquiring property for themselves at the expense of the politically weak. In real-world politics, the use of eminent domain is more likely to be determined by the relative power of the opposing interests than by the presence or absence of genuine holdout problems.

Secret assembly may not work well as a tool for acquiring land for government-owned projects. When government funds are spent, there is a strong case for transparency in order to facilitate public debate.[65]

But it is generally effective for privately owned development projects of the sort at issue in *Kelo* and most other blight and economic development takings.

III. Why Post-Kelo Eminent Domain Reform is Not Enough

The Supreme Court's controversial decision in *Kelo v. City ofNew London* generated a massive political backlash that some believe has greatly diminished the problem of eminent domain abuse. *Kelo* was one of the most unpopular Supreme Court decisions in history, with polls showing that over 80 percent of the public opposing the ruling.[66] As a result, forty-three states[67] and the federal government enacted legislation intended to curb economic development takings in the years since *Kelo.*[68]

Unfortunately, the majority of the new reform laws are likely to be ineffective, imposing few or no meaningful constraints on the use of eminent domain.[69] Many of them forbid takings that transfer property to private parties for "economic development," but allow virtually identical condemnations to continue under other names. For example, numerous states continue to allow "blight" condemnations under definitions of blight so broad that virtually any area qualifies.[70]

Many of the states that have enacted ineffective post-*Kelo* reforms or no reforms at all are among those that make the most extensive use of eminent domain for the benefit of private interests.[71] They include such large states as California, New York, New Jersey, and Texas.[72] The ineffectiveness of many post*Kelo* reforms is in part caused by public ignorance. Survey data shows that only about 13 percent of Americans know whether their state has enacted a post-*Kelo* eminent domain reform law and whether that law is likely to be effective or not.[73] Public ignorance enables state legislators to satisfy public demand for action on eminent domain without adopting laws that genuinely constrain blight and economic development takings.

Some real progress has been made as a result of the *Kelo* backlash. Four states—most notably Florida — now forbid both "blight" and economic development condemnations completely, and about fifteen others have banned economic development takings and defined blight narrowly.[74] These are important gains. But they do not go far enough. Poor minorities are still vulnerable to eminent domain abuse in most states.

This is most clearly the case in those states where post-*Kelo* reform laws impose no meaningful constraints on the range of properties that can be condemned. But even those reform laws that define "blight" narrowly still leave many of the minority poor at risk. Even a narrow definition of blight—one that encompasses only areas with conditions that pose a genuine threat to public health or safety—would still encompass many inner city neighborhoods. And such areas are disproportionately inhabited by the minority poor. Professor David Beito's testimony at this hearing gives an indication of the sorts of abuses that can occur even in a state that has enacted a relatively strong post-*Kelo* reform law.[75]

The alleviation of genuine blight is a proper objective of public policy. But, in most cases, it does not require the use of eminent domain. We need not destroy blighted neighborhoods in order to save them. A much better approach is the use of nuisance law or targeted public health regulations to eliminate dangerous conditions without expelling the people who live in the area.[76] In the long run, the best solution to urban blight is economic growth. And such growth is more likely to occur if the authorities respect the property rights of the poor, thereby incentivizing productive investment.[77] Growth is unlikely to flourish in neighborhoods where residents live in fear of condemnation.

Conclusion

For decades, eminent domain has been used and abused in ways that victimize minority groups, especially the minority poor. In recent years, state court decisions and eminent domain reform laws have partially addressed this longstanding problem. Nonetheless, much remains to be done before the property rights of minorities—and all Americans—are fully secure. Stronger eminent domain reform laws are needed at both the state and federal levels. For their part, the courts must give property rights protection equal to that afforded other constitutional rights.

J. Peter Byrne, Professor of Law, Georgetown University Law Center

Eminent Domain and Racial Discrimination: A Bogus Equation

This hearing addresses claims that the use of eminent domain for economic development unfairly and disproportionately harms racial and ethnic minorities. These claims draw on the history of urban renewal prior to the 1960s, when many African Americans and others were displaced by publicly funded projects that bulldozed their homes in largely failed attempts to modernize cities. Justice Clarence Thomas's dissent in *Kelo v. City of New London* further argued that the use of eminent domain for economic redevelopment would inevitably harm minorities and the poor.[1]

Such concerns in our time are seriously misplaced. Redevelopment projects using eminent domain continue to be an invaluable tool for maintaining the economic competitiveness and livability of urban areas where property ownership is fragmented and where minorities live in large numbers. The discriminatory elements of older urban renewal reflect the racism generally prevalent in political life in the 1940s and '50s, and have been largely eliminated by the growth of political power by African Americans and other urban minorities, as well as the changed fiscal relations between the federal and local governments, the effect of which has been to give greater control over redevelopment projects to local political leaders. Use of eminent domain, rarely now applied to residences, today requires political consent and community buy-in.

Eminent domain is a crucial legislative power exercised by governments around the world and dating back at least to Roman times. It empowers government to acquire property in specific locations for the construction of networks and the assembly of large tracts even when private owners do not wish to sell or holdout for excessive payment. Under our constitution, owners are protected by the requirement that government pay them "just compensation." The meaning of the Takings Clause of the Fifth Amendment relating to taking property for "public use" long has been controversial, but no U.S. Supreme Court decision contradicts the holding of *Kelo* that public use includes publicly approved condemnations for economic redevelopment of economically distressed areas. The quality of the redevelopment projects varies, but recent successful projects can be found from the Ferry Building in San Francisco to Times Square in New York.[2] Economic revitalization of urban areas will tend to aid poor minorities who disproportionately dwell in cities, by increasing employment and tax revenues for education and other city services.

Political realities have changed dramatically since the urban renewal period. Minorities have secured significant political power in nearly every U.S. city, as well as increased influence in private real estate markets. Redevelopment projects have largely come under the control of local governments, as federal money and direction have disappeared. Local officials strive to avoid displacement of homes because of negative political repercussions and expensive litigation. Federal and state statutes have in many instances increased the payments due property owners above what "just compensation" requires. In these circumstances, the condemnation of homes is rare and has little or no identifiable ethnic or racial character. The plaintiffs in *Kelo* were white, middle class people—which explains a good bit of the hysterical media reaction.

The changes in the political economy of economic development can be seen by comparing the urban renewal of Southwest Washington, DC, in the 1950s, approved by the Supreme Court in *Berman v. Parker*,[3] with the use of condemnation in DC today. The massive condemnations, bulldozing, and reconstruction of Southwest Washington comprised a complex episode with many facets, but poor African Americans residents seem to have suffered disproportionate displacement. At that time, there was no democracy or elected government at all in Washington; the statute authorizing the project was enacted by Congress, and the members of the Redevelopment Land Agency that carried out the project were appointed by the federal government or their DC appointees. The most controversial exercise of eminent domain in Washington D C in the past decade has been the condemnation of stores in the Skyland strip mall in Anacostia to permit the construction of a badly needed private supermarket for an underserved area. That action, although bitterly contested in court by some owners, was supported by many members of the local community, specifically approved by the DC Council, which was majority African American, and signed by Mayor Anthony Williams.[4] Although specifically exercised in order to convey the land to a private developer, it would be absurd to suggest that the case presents a civil rights issue appropriate for consideration by the U.S. Civil Rights Commission. Similar observations can be made about the use of eminent domain by Dudley Street Neighborhood Initiative in Boston to assemble land for affordable housing.[5]

Nor is there reason to suppose that condemnations for economic development are more likely to harm minorities than condemnations for other traditional public uses. Many of the most brutal condemnations in the urban renewal period were accomplished for highways and public housing where the government would actually own the site. Government has the same general incentive to seek less expensive or flourishing lands for condemnation whatever the use to be made. If the goal really is to protect minorities, why are the proponents not seeking to constrain the uses of eminent domain that historically have been most harmful to minorities? Yet, legislation recently introduced in Congress, H.R. 1433, ignores these exercises of eminent domain for highway construction and other public projects, while prohibiting economic development that has the potential to aid low income people.

The case against eminent domain here has been advanced largely on the basis of advocacy by libertarian organizations, which broadly oppose the use of eminent domain because they value private property more highly than local democracy. The evidence that that they marshal, such as the lurid *Victimizing the Vulnerable*, presents ambiguous data in highly colored language. That study shows no more than that communities are somewhat more likely to pursue redevelopment in poorer areas than in more affluent areas. There is no consideration of the public benefits to be gained from these projects, the distribution of such benefits, or the scope or character of citizen participation in decision making. Nonetheless, the study leaps to the astounding conclusion that, "The only real solution is prohibiting the use of eminent domain for private development to protect the constitutional rights of all citizens,...."[6] Thus, they oppose condemnation of the property of our largest corporations as much as that of the most economically marginal minority individual. The concern for the latter seems frankly tactical, since they know that they would get little hearing in many quarters simply advocating to reduce the scope of state legislative power over private property.

If one were worried about disproportionate impacts of eminent domain on the poor or minorities, there are remedies that would address that directly. One might provide more procedural protections or compensation to residents than to commercial property owners. One could mandate minimum payments to tenants, who normally receive no compensation when rental housing is condemned. The Fair Housing Act could be amended to clarify that it applies to condemnation of residences without regard to intent.[7] These ideas are all worthy of study but have not been because they do not meet the agenda of the libertarian groups driving the issue, which is to limit further the powers of government in favor of private capital. Proponents rather would deprive the DC government of the power to use eminent domain to build a supermarket in Anacostia. In a world of growing economic inequality, in a political climate demanding cutting taxes as well as medical and pension benefits, it is unfortunate we are spending this time discussing the non-issue of the effects of eminent domain on minorities.

Hilary O. Shelton, Director, NAACP Washington Bureau & Senior Vice-President for Advocacy and Policy

The Civil Rights Implications ofEminent Domain Abuse

Thank you, Chairman Castro and ladies and gentlemen of the Commission for inviting me here today to talk about property rights and the civil rights implications of eminent domain abuse.

My name is Hilary Shelton and I am the Director of the NAACP Washington Bureau and the Senior VP for Advocacy and Policy. The NAACP is our Nation's oldest, largest and most widely recognized grassroots-based civil rights organization. We currently have more than 2,200 units in every state in our country. The NAACP Washington Bureau is our national public policy and federal legislative advocacy arm.

Given our Nation's sad history of racial prejudice, racism, bigotry, and a basic disregard on the part of too many elected and appointed officials to the concerns and rights of racial and ethnic minority Americans, it should come as no surprise that eminent domain has been misused for centuries against African Americans and other racial and ethnic minorities, and the economically disadvantaged, at highly disproportionate rates.

Although nobody knows the exact numbers of people displaced through eminent domain across the nation, everyone seems to agree that African Americans are disproportionately affected. One source cites that since World War II, it is estimated that between 3 and 4 million Americans have been forcibly displaced from their homes as a result of urban renewal takings. It should surprise nobody that a vast majority of these people are racial and ethnic minorities.[1] Another says that ""[b]etween 1949 and 1973 ... 2,532 projects were carried out in 992 cities that displaced one million people, two-thirds of them African American," making African Americans, "five times more likely to be displaced than they should have been given their numbers in the population.[2]"

The NAACP has a deeply held concern that the newly sanctioned expansion of the use of eminent domain to allow the government or its designee to take property simply by asserting that it can put the property to a higher use, as was approved by the U.S. Supreme Court in its 2005 *Kelo v. City of New London* decision, will systemically sanction easier transfers of property, wealth, and community stability from those with less resources to those with more.

The history of eminent domain is rife with abuse specifically targeting racial and ethnic minority and poor neighborhoods. Indeed, the displacement of African Americans and urban renewal projects are so intertwined that "urban renewal" was often referred to as "black removal." Sadly, racial and ethnic minorities are not just affected more often by the exercise of eminent domain power, but we are almost always affected differently and more profoundly.

The vast disparities of African Americans or other racial or ethnic minorities who have been removed from their homes due to eminent domain actions is well documented.

A 2004 study estimated that 1,600 African American neighborhoods were destroyed by municipal projects in Los Angeles.[3] In San Jose, California, 95 percent of the properties targeted for economic redevelopment are Hispanic or Asian-owned, despite the fact that only 30 percent of businesses in that area are owned by racial or ethnic minorities.[4] In Mt. Holly Township, New Jersey, officials have targeted for economic redevelopment a neighborhood in which the percentage of African American residents, 44 percent, is twice that of the entire township and nearly triple that of Burlington County. In 2004, the city of Alabaster, AL, used "blight" as a pretext to take 400 acres of rural property, much of it owned by low-income African Americans, for a new super-sized mega department store. Many of the residents had lived there for generations, and two other super-sized mega department stores owned by the same company were located less than fifteen miles away. Several of the landowners, particularly those who lacked economic resources, political clout, and legal aid, ended up selling out at an unfair discount. According to a 1989 study 90 percent of the 10,000 families displaced by highway projects in Baltimore, Maryland, were African Americans.[5]

The motives behind the disparities are varied. Many of the studies I mentioned in the previous examples contend that the goal of many of these displacements is to segregate and maintain the isolation of poor, minority and otherwise outcast populations. Furthermore, condemnations in low-income or predominantly racial and ethnic minority neighborhoods are often easier to accomplish because these groups are less likely, or often unable, to effectively contest the action either politically or in our nation's courts.

Lastly, municipalities often look for areas with low property values when deciding where to pursue redevelopment projects because it costs the condemning authority less and thus the state or local government gains more, financially, when they replace areas of low property values with those with higher property values. Thus, even if you dismiss all other motivations, allowing municipalities to pursue eminent domain for private development as was upheld by the U.S. Supreme Court in *Kelo* will clearly perpetuate, if not exacerbate, the disparate impact on African Americans and other racial and ethnic minorities, and the economically disadvantaged in our country.

As I said at the beginning of my testimony, not only are African Americans and other racial and ethnic minorities more likely to be subject to eminent domain, but the negative impact of these takings on these men, women and families is much more severe.

First, the term "just compensation," when used in eminent domain cases, is almost always a misnomer. The fact that a particular property is identified and designated for "economic development" almost certainly means that the market is currently undervaluing that property or that the property has some "trapped" value that the market is not yet recognizing.

Moreover, when an area is taken for "economic development," low-income families are driven out of their communities and find that they cannot afford to live in the "revitalized" neighborhoods; the remaining "affordable" housing in the area is almost certain to become less so. When the goal is to increase the area's tax base, it only makes sense that the previous low-income residents will not be able to remain in the area. This is borne out not only by common sense, but also by statistics: one study from the mid-1980s showed that 86 percent of those relocated by an exercise of the eminent domain power were paying more rent at their new residences, with the median rent almost doubling.[6]

Furthermore, to the extent that such exercise of the takings power is more likely to occur in areas with significant racial and ethnic minority populations, and even assuming a proper motive on the part of the government, the effect will likely be to destabilize organized minority communities. This dispersion both eliminates, or at the very least drastically undermines, established community support mechanisms and has a deleterious effect on these communities' ability to exercise what little political power they may have established. In fact, the very threat of such takings will also hinder the development of stronger ethnic and racial minority communities. The incentive to invest in one's own community, financially and otherwise, directly correlates with confidence in one's ability to realize the fruits of such efforts.

By broadening the permissible uses of eminent domain in a way that is not limited by specific criteria, many minority neighborhoods will be at increased risk of having property taken. Individuals in those areas will thus have even less incentive to engage in community-building and improvement for fear that such efforts will be wasted.

In conclusion, allow me to reiterate that by allowing pure economic development motives to constitute public use for eminent domain purposes, state and local governments will now infringe on the property rights of those with less economic and political power with more regularity. And, as I have testified today, these groups, low-income Americans, and a disparate number of African Americans and other racial and ethnic minority Americans, are the least able to bear this burden.

As I have discussed in my testimony, too many of our communities--racial and ethnic minorities, the elderly, and the low-income--have witnessed an abuse of eminent domain powers that has too often been devastating. Given the numerous chronicles of abuse, it is the hope of the NAACP that all responses, legislative, administrative and other, to address eminent domain abuse be educated and well informed by our shared history. We need to ensure that certain segments of our population that have too long been muted in this takings issue have a voice. We need to understand how it has been too easy to exploit these communities by imposing eminent domain not only in the pursuit of economic development but also in the name of addressing "blight." We also need to make sure that any compensation is fair and will not result in forcing those being displaced to accept less than they had.

Historically and today, it has been too easy to characterize minority, elderly, or low-income communities as "blighted" for eminent domain purposes and subject them to the will of the government. If proposals contain language that could potentially exclude these communities from protection against eminent domain abuses, we have failed in our responsibility to serve and give a voice to this constituency which has already been, and continues to be, abused.

Additionally, in considering the interests of our communities, we raise a broader concern regarding the use of eminent domain for any purpose, including those purposes traditionally viewed as "public purposes," such as highways, utilities, and waste disposal. Even these more traditional uses of eminent domain have disproportionately burdened those communities with the least political power—the poor, minorities, and working class families. Furthermore, it is not only our owners that suffer, but our renters, whether they are residents or proprietors of small businesses, who are provided no protections and pay a heavy and uncompensated price when eminent domain is imposed.

For these reasons, as the majority in *Kelo* suggested, there must be sufficient process protections for minority communities, regardless of the purpose and however beneficial to the public. The process must be open and the participation of the potentially impacted community needs to be guaranteed, as well as fair compensation. This is the voice that our communities, that all American communities, deserve.

Thank you again, Chairman Castro and Commission members, for allowing me to testify before you today about the NAACP position on the civil rights implications of eminent domain abuse.

The NAACP stands ready to work with federal, state and local municipality officials to develop policy and legislation to end eminent domain abuse while focusing on real community development concerns like building safe, clean, and affordable housing in communities with good public schools, an effective accessible high quality health care system, small business development and growth, and a significant available living wage job pool.

Thank you very much and I look forward to your questions and our discussion.

David Beito, Chair, U.S. Commission on Civil Rights' Alabama State Advisory Committee

Eminent Domain through the Back Door in Montgomery, Alabama[1]

Thank you for inviting me here today. Let me start by saying that I speak for myself in this testimony, not the Alabama State Advisory Committee, which I chair. I have little to add to Ilya Somin's insightful and well-researched overview, and agree with the main thrust of his argument. As Somin points out, Americans into the early twentieth century greatly appreciated the link between civil rights and property rights. Civil rights champions ranging from the earliest abolitionists to the founders of the NAACP emphasized the constitutional protection of the right to acquire and hold property as essential to the economic progress of the poor and oppressed. In 1849, for example, Frederick Douglass declared that "civil government" should be "solemnly bound to protect the weak against the strong, the oppressed against the oppressor, the few against the many, and to secure the humblest subject in the full possession of his rights of person and of property." In defending property rights, of course, Douglass made a distinction between property originally acquired through mutual consent and homesteading, which he regarded as legitimate, and "property in man" which he viewed as "man-stealing."[2]

Rather than revisit these broader historical issues, or even eminent domain as conventionally understood, my testimony will highlight a generally overlooked threat to the property rights of the poor and vulnerable. For lack of a better term, this threat can be called "eminent domain through the back door." I first encountered this phenomenon after becoming chair of the Alabama State Advisory Committee for the U.S. Commission on Civil Rights. Our Committee took seriously the mandate of the national Commission to look creatively and expansively at civil rights issues. One of our members, Margaret Brown, suggested that we examine the impact on state and local government policy on the property rights of minorities.

Not long before our Committee took on this issue, the U.S. Supreme Court had handed down its landmark decision in 2005 of *Kelo v. New London.* This ruling was highly permissive to local governments seeking to take property for economic development. In response to the "post-*Kelo* backlash," more than forty states enacted laws to protect property owners and narrow the discretion of governments. One of the first was Alabama's law of 2005 (followed up by another, more restrictive law, in 2006), which prohibited the use of conventional eminent domain for economic development.[3]

All of our members, regardless of partisanship, ideology, or race, agreed on the need to pursue the issue. As a result, the Advisory Committee convened two public forums. The first was in 2008 at the historic 16th Street Baptist Church in Birmingham, Alabama. The church was an early meeting place for civil rights activists. In 1963, it was the scene of a tragic bombing which resulted in the deaths of four school children. During our meeting, several citizens from around the state came forward to share their grievances about property rights abuse. One of these was Jim Peera, a developer in Montgomery, whose family had left Africa in the 1970s because of persecution of Asian minorities. Peera recounted disturbing examples of how blacks in Montgomery, a city often called the cradle of civil rights, were losing their property through an extensive application of Section 11-53B-1 *et. seq.* of the Alabama code. This provision leaves a major loophole for the indirect taking of property outside of conventional eminent domain. The legislature did not repeal it as part of its post-*Kelo* eminent domain reforms.[4]

The first two paragraphs of 11-53B-1 *et. seq.* give some sense of its permissive nature:

> "It is estimated that within the municipalities of the state, there exist several thousand parcels of real property that due to poor design, obsolescence, or neglect, have become unsafe to the extent of becoming public nuisances. Much of this property is vacant or in a state of disrepair and is causing or may cause a blight or blighting influence on the city and the

> neighborhoods in which the property is located. Such property constitutes a threat to the health, safety, and welfare to the citizens of the state and is an impediment to economic development within the municipality. ... It is the intent of this chapter to authorize a municipality of the state to proceed with the demolition or repair of a structure based on its own findings, and to set out a method for collecting the assessment liens so imposed."[5]

In contrast to the standard eminent domain process, Montgomery property owners on the receiving end of Section 11-53B-1 *et. seq.* do not have any right to compensation, even in theory. Once declaring the property a nuisance, the city typically demolishes the structure and then bills the owner, often by slapping a lien on the property, for the costs of demolition including the carting away of the rubble. As Peera pointed out, because the owners are often poor, many cannot afford to pay and thus have to sell or abandon the land. He charged that the city was demolishing buildings which, by any reasonably objective standard, were neither blighted nor a nuisance. Of course, this point is somewhat academic since Alabama law gives governments maximum leeway to interpret the standards of blight and nuisance as well as to selectively apply them.[6]

Peera's information played a key role in convincing the Alabama State Advisory Committee to call a second public forum in April 2009 to focus on the situation in Montgomery. During that meeting, Peera showed the audience a map of demolitions in a single year. Most were in a small area in Montgomery's most heavily black areas, including Rosa Park's old neighborhood. There were more than fifty demolitions in 2008. The city council approved 29 more in 2009, 62 in 2010, and 18 by the end of March 2011. Most notably, at this meeting, Peera also told us about the case of Jimmie McCall who, as a result, testified.[7]

In his willingness to fight city hall, McCall was a rarity among Montgomery's property owners threatened with demolition of their homes. He has lived in the city for several decades. For years, he has scraped together a living by salvaging rare materials from historic homes and then selling them to private builders. Sometimes months went by before he had a client. Finally, he had put aside enough to purchase two acres in Montgomery and started to build. He did the work himself using materials accumulated in his business including a supply of sturdy and extremely rare longleaf pine.[8]

McCall only earned enough money to build in incremental stages but eventually his "dream house" took shape. From the outset, however, the city showed unremitting hostility. He almost lost count of the roadblocks it threw up including a citation for keeping the necessary building materials on his own land during the construction process. More seriously, in 2007 he was charged under Section 11-B-1 *et. seq.* on the grounds that his home, then under construction, was a nuisance.[9]

The reaction of Montgomery's city fathers seemed strange to McCall. Wasn't he trying to fight blight by building a new home? McCall suspects that wealthy developers are trying to get their hands on the property: a rare two-acre parcel on a major thoroughfare. Unlike countless others in similar straits, McCall fought back and hired an experienced local lawyer. He negotiated a court-enforced agreement which gave him eighteen months to complete the home. Only a month after the agreement took effect in 2008, the city demolished the structure. Local bureaucrats, obviously in a hurry, did not give him notice when they sent in the bulldozers on the same day as the court order authorizing them. McCall appealed to the same judge who had allowed the demolition. Stating that she had been misled, she ordered the city to pay compensation. Montgomery has appealed and at this writing McCall has not received a cent. McCall thinks that the city intends to drag it out until his money runs out.[10]

On April 15, 2010, I received a phone call from Karen Jones, another black property owner from Montgomery. She related a case which was no less compelling than that of McCall's. Only a day before she called me, the city had demolished her family home including furniture, a family bible, and old photographs. The authorities charged the property was a nuisance because the front porch was in disrepair. Although the city mailed out notices before sending out the bulldozers, none of them went to Jones. Instead they went to Forie Jones, her grandmother (deceased in 1989) and Matthew Jones, her uncle (deceased in 2000).[11]

The city claimed then, and now, that Karen Jones is not the owner although she pays the property taxes (which were not in arrears) and has a warranty deed from 1982 indicating that she is an heir. Apparently, all of the other family members support her decision. Despite asserting that Jones is not the owner, the city has billed her more than $1,200 for the costs of demolition. Jones refused, and continues to refuse, to pay the lien on principle. In May of this year, the city tried to sell the property at auction, still naming the deceased Forie Jones as the owner in the official online information describing the property. According to Karen Jones, there were no bidders. She charges that the city has taken no action against other properties in the city which are in much greater states of disrepair. Partly as a result of the Jones case, the Castle

Coalition of the Institute for Justice, a leading force against eminent domain abuse, has taken a special interest in the Montgomery situation.[12]

As Ilya Somin points out, many state laws, including that of Alabama, are still woefully inadequate in the protection of individual rights under eminent domain. I also second his emphasis on the need for local governments to work with property owners rather than adopt an adversarial relationship. Reforms will accomplish little, however, if they fail to address those abuses that occur outside of the conventional eminent domain framework. Under eminent domain through the back door, governments never actually try to take the land, at least at the beginning of the process, but the end result is often the same or worse for property owners. If they are poor and do not have access to good legal representation, they will often have to either sell or abandon their property—that is after it has become nothing more than a vacant lot. As legal restrictions on conventional eminent domain become tougher, it becomes even more likely that governments will exploit this loophole.

Any reforms to eminent domain through the back door should start with the assumption that the property rights of the poor are just as worthy of protection as those of the rich. Put another way, it is essential that these individual rights be respected as ends in themselves not merely as a means to further the ends of another person or group. For this reason, these reforms should make it clear that the burden of proof is on local governments, not the property owner, to show that a genuine nuisance, which must be narrowly and specifically defined, exists.

Of course, any reforms should assume that the onus be placed on governments to fully inform the actual property owner of his or her rights prior to any demolition. There should be no more cases like those of Karen Jones and Jimmie McCall and, if there are, local governments should be required to pay full compensation for any mistake and those responsible should be prosecuted. To put teeth in these reforms, each state could create a property rights ombudsperson in the attorney general's office. The role of the ombudsperson will be to provide owners with an informational brochure written in clear and concise language explaining their rights and, if necessary, recommend that the state bring charges against the local governments in cases of abuse.[13]

Lastly, I strongly recommend that this Commission call a special meeting to be devoted solely to the situation in Montgomery. In my view, unless this happens, the city will continue a policy of obfuscation and delay. I suggest that Mayor Todd Strange, who did not respond to invitations from the Commission to be here today, be at the top of any invitation list along with such alleged victims of property rights abuse via eminent domain through the back door as Karen Jones, Jim Peera, and Jimmie McCall.

Especially during a time of recession and tumbling home prices, local and state governments should regard the existing property owners in lower-income neighborhoods in Montgomery and elsewhere as their allies and assets to the community. They will have a great deal more success with economic development if they treat these owners as valuable urban pioneers who deserve praise and encouragement rather than as obstacles to be pushed out of the way if their rights conflict with some broader social and economic agenda.

PANELISTS' BIOGRAPHIES

Ilya Somin

Ilya Somin is a Professor at George Mason University School of Law. His research focuses on constitutional law, property law, and the study of popular political participation and its implications for constitutional democracy. Somin currently serves as co-editor of the *Supreme Court Economic Review,* one of the country's top-rated law and economics journals. His work has appeared in numerous scholarly journals and popular press outlets, including the *Yale Law Journal*, *Stanford Law Review*, *Northwestern University Law Review*, *Los Angeles Times*, *National Law Journal,* and *Reason*. His amicus brief on behalf of urban planning scholar Jane Jacobs was cited by the Supreme Court in its majority opinion in *Kelo v. City ofNew London*. In July 2009, he testified on property rights issues at the United States Senate Judiciary Committee confirmation hearings for Supreme Court Justice Sonia Sotomayor. Somin writes regularly for the popular *Volokh Conspiracy* law and politics blog.

During the Fall 2008 semester, he served as visiting professor of law at the University of Pennsylvania Law School. Somin has previously been a visiting professor at the University of Hamburg, Germany, and the University of Torcuato Di Tella in Buenos Aires, Argentina. Before joining the faculty at George Mason, he was the John M. Olin Fellow in Law at Northwestern University Law School in 2002–2003. In 2001–2002, he clerked for the Hon. Judge Jerry E. Smith of the U.S. Court of Appeals for the Fifth Circuit. Professor Somin earned his B.A., *Summa Cum Laude*, at Amherst College, M.A. in Political Science from Harvard University, and J.D. from Yale Law School.

J. Peter Byrne

J. Peter Byrne is Professor of Law at the Georgetown University Law Center. He teaches Property, Land Use, Historic Preservation, and Constitutional Law. Professor Byrne holds degrees from Northwestern University and from the University of Virginia School of Law. He was a law clerk to Chief Judge Frank Coffin of the U.S. Court of Appeals for the First Circuit and for Associate Justice Lewis F. Powell, Jr. of the U.S. Supreme Court; he practiced law with the DC firm of Covington and Burling. Professor Byrne has taught at Georgetown since 1985 and served as Associate Dean from 1997 until 2000. He currently is Faculty Director of the Georgetown Climate Center and of the Georgetown Environmental Law and Policy Program. Professor Byrne has published numerous law journal articles on Land Use and Property topics and is currently writing a book on Historic Preservation Law.

Hilary O. Shelton

Hilary O. Shelton presently serves as the Senior *Vice President for Advocacy and Policy/Director to the NAACP's Washington Bureau.* The Washington Bureau is the Federal legislative and national public policy division of the over 500,000-member, 2,200-membership unit, national civil rights organization. In this capacity, Mr. Shelton is responsible for advocating the federal public policy issue agenda of the oldest, largest, and most widely-recognized civil rights organization in the United States to the U.S. Government. His government affairs portfolio includes crucial issues such as affirmative action, equal employment protection, access to quality education, stopping gun violence, ending racial profiling, abolition of the death penalty, access to comprehensive healthcare, voting rights protection, federal sentencing reform, and a host of civil rights enforcement, expansion, and protection issues.

Prior to serving as director to the NAACP Washington Bureau, Mr. Shelton served in the position of *Federal Liaison/Assistant Director* to the Government Affairs Department of *The College Fund/UNCF*, also known as *The United Negro College Fund* in Washington, DC. In this capacity, Mr. Shelton worked with Senate and House Members of the U.S. Congress, Federal Agencies and Departments, college and university presidents and faculty members, as well as the White House and various government agencies to secure the survival, growth and educational programming excellence of the 40 private historically black colleges and universities throughout the United States.

Mr. Shelton serves on a number of national boards of directors, including The Leadership Conference on Civil Rights, The Center for Democratic Renewal, and the Congressional Black Caucus Institute among many others. He has received a number of awards and recognitions for his unwavering dedication to the mission and goals of the NAACP. Among these, Mr. Shelton is the proud recipient of the *National NAACP Medgar W. Evers Award for Excellence*, the highest honor bestowed upon a national professional staff member of the NAACP, as well as the *Congressional Black Caucus' Chairman's Award.* He holds degrees in political science, communications, and legal studies from Howard University in Washington, DC, the University of Missouri in St. Louis, and Northeastern University in Boston, Massachusetts, respectively.

David Beito

David T. Beito is a professor at the University of Alabama. He is the author of *Taxpayers in Revolt: Tax Resistance during the Great Depression* (Chapel Hill: University of North Carolina Press, 1989), *From Mutual Aid to the Welfare State: Fraternal Societies and Social Services, 1890–1967* (Chapel Hill: University of North Carolina Press, 2000); and *Black Maverick: T.R.M. Howard's Fight for Civil Rights and Economic Power* (Urbana: University of Illinois Press, 2009). The last book focuses on Dr. T.R.M. Howard who was not only one of the wealthiest blacks in Mississippi but was also the main early civil rights mentor to Medgar Evers and Fannie Lou Hamer.

Professor Beito edited *The Voluntary City: Choice, Community, and Civil Society* (Ann Arbor: University of Michigan Press, 2002). He has a book under contract with the University of Illinois Press entitled *"The Richer Gift ofIndividualism:" The Political Writings ofZora Neale Hurston.*

Professor Beito has published in the *Journal of Interdisciplinary History, Journal of Policy History, Journal of Southern History,* and *Journal of Urban History* among other scholarly journals. He has received fellowships from the Earhart Foundation, the Olin Foundation, and the Institute for Humane Studies. He has also published articles in *The Wall Street Journal*, *The Los Angeles Times*, *Reason*, and *American Enterprise*. His most recent articles (both in *The Wall Street Journal* in 2011) focused on the overlooked nationwide tax revolt of the 1930s and the provision of decentralized relief after the Tuscaloosa tornado of 2011.

Professor Beito edits the *Liberty and Power Blog* at the History News Network and is chair of the Alabama State Advisory Committee of the U.S. Commission on Civil Rights.

End Notes for Executive Summary

[1] "Nor shall private property be taken for public use, without just compensation." U.S. CONST. amend. V.

[2] 348 U.S. 26 (1954).

[3] David Beito and Ilya Somin, "Battle Over Eminent Domain is Another Civil Rights Issue," *Kansas City Star*, Apr. 27, 2008, *available at* http://www.cato.org/pub display.php?pub id=9361.

[4] *See* Dick M. Carpenter and John K. Ross, Institute for Justice, *Victimizing the Vulnerable: The Demographics ofEminent Domain Abuse*, June 2007, p. 3.

[5] Brief for Nat'l Ass'n for the Advancement of Colored People et al. as Amici Curiae Supporting Petitioners at 7, in *Kelo v. New London,* 545 U.S. 469 (2005) (No. 04-108), *available at* http://www.ij.org/images/pdf_folder/private_property/kelo/naacp02.pdf.

[6] *See id.* (citing Wendell E. Pritchett, *The "Public Menace" ofBlight: Urban Renewal and the Private Uses ofEminent Domain*, 21 YALE L. & POL'Y REV. 1, 6 (2003)).

[7] 545 U.S. 469 (2005).

[8] *See, e.g., id.* at 521 (Thomas, J., dissenting) ("Allowing the government to take property solely for public purposes is bad enough, but extending the concept of public purpose to encompass any economically beneficial goal guarantees that these losses will fall disproportionately on poor communities."); *see also id.* at 505 (O'Connor, J., dissenting).

[9] Carpenter and Ross, *Victimizing the Vulnerable*, p. 7.

[10] Although the number was 43 when the Commission held its briefing on August 12, 2011, it has increased to 44 since then.

[11] *See, e.g.*, Beito and Somin, *Battle Over Eminent Domain.*

End Notes for Summary of Proceedings

[1] Ilya Somin, Testimony, *Briefing Before the U.S. Commission on Civil Rights*, Washington, DC, Aug. 12, 2011, transcript, p. 9 (hereafter cited as *Briefing Transcript*), *available at* http://www.usccr.gov/calendar/trnscrpt/08-12-11ccr1.pdf.

[2] Ibid., pp. 10-11.

[3] Ibid., pp. 9-11.

[4] Ibid., pp. 11-12.

[5] Ibid., pp. 9, 12.

[6] Ibid., pp. 12-13.

[7] Ibid., pp. 13-15.

[8] Ibid., pp. 14-15.

[9] Ibid., p. 15.

[10] Ibid., pp. 15-16.

[11] Ibid., p. 16.

[12] Ibid., pp. 16-17.

[13] As noted earlier, 43 states had such reforms at the time of the Commission's August 2011 briefing. Today, 44 states have enacted reforms. *See, for example,* The Eminent Domain Blog, "Proposed Legislation Seeks to Amend New Jersey's Redevelopment Law Limiting the Abuse," Mar. 26, 2013, http://ownerscounsel.blogspot.com/2013/03/proposed-legislation-seeks-toamend-new.html, which suggests that New Jersey may soon be the 45th state restricting takings.

[14] Ibid., p. 17.

[15] Ibid., pp. 15, 17.

[16] Ibid., pp. 17-18.

[17] J. Peter Byrne Testimony, *Briefing Transcript*, p. 20.

[18] Ibid., p. 20.

[19] Ibid., pp. 18-19.

[20] Ibid., p. 19.

[21] Ibid., pp. 19-21.

[22] Ibid., pp. 20-21.

[23] Ibid., p. 21.

[24] Ibid., p. 22.

[25] Ibid., pp. 22-23. In a public comment submitted to the Commission after the briefing, Elaine J. Mittleman, an attorney representing several displaced property and small-business owners in the Skyland project, stated "the Skyland project is not designed to provide a supermarket. There is an existing Safeway across the street from Skyland." Elaine J. Mittleman, *Statement submitted to the United States Commission on Civil Rights Concerning the Civil Rights Implications ofEminent Domain*, Sept. 9, 2011, p. 3.

[26] Byrne Testimony, *Briefing Transcript*, p. 23.

[27] Ibid., pp. 23-24.

[28] Ibid., p. 24.

[29] Private Property Rights Protection Act of 2011, H.R. 1433, 112th Cong. (2011).

[30] Byrne Testimony, *Briefing Transcript*, p. 24.

[31] *See* Carpenter and Ross, *Victimizing the Vulnerable*, p. 7.

[32] Byrne Testimony, *Briefing Transcript*, pp. 24-25.

[33] Ibid., p. 25.

[34] Ibid., pp. 25-26.

[35] Ibid., p. 26.

[36] Hilary Shelton Testimony, *Briefing Transcript*, p. 27.

[37] Ibid., pp. 27-28.

[38] *See* David Bieto and Ilya Somin, "Battle Over Eminent Domain is Another Civil Rights Issue," *The Kansas City Star,* Apr. 27, 2008, *available at* http://www.cato.org/pub_display.php?pub_id=9361.

[39] *See* Mindy Thompson Fullilove, *What is the Price of the Commons?* Feb. 2007.

[40] Shelton Testimony, *Briefing Transcript*, pp. 28-29.

[41] Ibid., pp. 28-29.

[42] Ibid., p. 30.

[43] Ibid., pp. 29-30.

[44] Ibid., pp. 29, 31.

[45] Ibid., p. 31.

[46] *See* Herbert J. Gans, *The Urban Villagers: Group and Class in the Life ofItalian Americans*, (The Free Press, 1982), p. 380.

[47] Shelton Testimony, *Briefing Transcript*, pp. 31-32.

[48] Ibid., p. 32.

[49] Ibid., pp. 32-33.

[50] Ibid., p. 33.

[51] Ibid., pp. 33-34.

[52] Ibid., pp. 33-34.

[53] Ibid., pp. 34-35.

[54] David Beito Testimony, *Briefing Transcript*, pp. 35-36.

[55] Ibid., p. 36.

[56] Ibid., p. 36.

[57] Ibid., pp. 36-37.

[58] Ibid., p. 37.

[59] "We hold the civil government to be solemnly bound to protect the weak against the strong, the oppressed against the oppressor, the few against the many, and to secure the humblest subject in the full possession of his rights of person and of property." Ibid., p. 38.

[60] Ibid., p. 38. Mr. Beito added that the quotation was not referring to the ownership of slaves, because Douglass believed that people owned themselves. Ibid.

[61] Ibid., pp. 40, 42.

[62] Ibid., pp. 38-40.

[63] Ibid., pp. 39-40.

[64] Ibid., pp. 40-41.

[65] Ibid., pp. 41-42.

[66] Ibid., p. 43.

[67] "[T]he powers not delegated to the United States by the Constitution, nor prohibited by it to the States, are reserved to the States respectively, or to the people." U.S. CONST. amend. X.

[68] "[N]or shall private property be taken for public use, without just compensation." U.S. CONST. amend. V.

[69] *Briefing Transcript*, pp. 44-45.

[70] Ibid., p. 45.

[71] Ibid., pp. 45-46.

[72] *United States v. Gettysburg Electric Ry. Co.*, 160 U.S. 668 (1896).

[73] *Briefing Transcript*, pp. 46-47.

[74] Ibid., p. 47.

[75] Ibid., pp. 47-48.

[76] Ibid., pp. 54-55.

[77] Ibid., p. 79.

[78] Ibid., pp. 48-49.

[79] Ibid., pp. 48-49.

[80] Ibid., p. 49.

[81] Ibid., p. 50.

[82] Ibid., pp. 50-51.

[83] Ibid., p. 51.

[84] [-Ed.] Professor Byrne first stated that the New London City Council determined that the city was blighted, and that the redevelopment program was an appropriate remedy for blight. Ibid., p. 51. In later discussion, Vice Chair Thernstrom questioned whether the homes in the

Kelo case were declared to be blighted. Ibid., p. 56. Professor Somin stated that the city government did not claim that the New London homes were blighted. Ibid., p. 57. Professor Somin further stated that the Supreme Court likely took the *Kelo* case because it was a pure economic development case with no allegation of blight. Ibid, p. 57. When Professor Byrne had another turn to address the Commission, he agreed that he had misspoken in implying that the *Kelo* case had a finding of blight. Ibid., p. 60.

[85] Ibid., p. 51.
[86] Ibid., pp. 51-52.
[87] Ibid., p. 52.
[88] Ibid., pp. 52-54.
[89] Ibid., p. 53.
[90] Ibid., p. 54.
[91] Ibid., p. 55.
[92] Ibid., pp. 55-56.
[93] Ibid., p. 22.
[94] Ibid., pp. 56-57.
[95] Ibid., pp. 57-58.
[96] Ibid., p. 58.
[97] Ibid., pp. 58-59.
[98] Ibid., p. 59.
[99] Ibid., pp. 59-60.
[100] Ibid., pp. 60-61.
[101] Ibid., p. 61.
[102] Ibid., p. 61.
[103] Ibid., p. 62.
[104] Ibid., pp. 62-63.
[105] Ibid., p. 63.
[106] Ibid., p. 63.
[107] Ibid., p. 64.
[108] Ibid., pp. 65-66.
[109] Ibid., p. 66.
[110] Ibid., pp. 66-67.
[111] Ibid., p. 67.
[112] Ibid., pp. 67-68.
[113] Ibid., pp. 68-69.
[114] Ibid., pp. 69-70.
[115] Ibid., p. 69.
[116] Ibid., p. 70.
[117] Ibid., p. 71.
[118] Ibid., pp. 71-72.
[119] Ibid., p. 73.
[120] Ibid., pp. 73-74.
[121] Ibid., p. 74.
[122] Ibid., pp. 74-75.
[123] Ibid., pp. 75-76.
[124] Ibid., p. 76.
[125] *City ofLas Vegas Downtown Redevelopment Agency v. Pappas*, 76 P.3d 1 (Nev. 2003).
[126] *Briefing Transcript*, p. 77.

[127] *See Hawaii Housing Auth. v. Midkiff*, 467 U.S. 229, 241 (1984).
[128] *Briefing Transcript*, pp. 77-78.
[129] Ibid., p. 78.
[130] Ibid., p. 78.
[131] Ibid., p. 79.
[132] Ibid., pp. 79-80.
[133] Ibid., p. 80.
[134] Ibid., pp. 80-81.
[135] Ibid., pp. 81, 82.
[136] Ibid., p. 82.
[137] Ibid., pp. 82-83.
[138] Ibid., p. 83.
[139] Ibid., pp. 83-84.
[140] *See* Carpenter and Ross, *Victimizing the Vulnerable.* The Carpenter and Ross article's appendix A describes the methodology of their study using 2000 Census data for block groups. *See* ibid., p. 9.
[141] *Briefing Transcript*, p. 84.

End Note for Commissioners' Statements and Rebuttals

[1] *The Lost Decade of the Middle Class: Fewer, Poorer, Gloomier,* Pew Research Social & Demographic Trends, http://www.pewsocialtrends.org/2012/08/22/the-lost-decade-of-the-middle-class/, in part, "For the middle-income group, the "lost decade" of the 2000s has been even worse for wealth loss than for income loss. The median income of the middle-income tier fell 5%, but median wealth (assets minus debt) declined by 28%, to $93,150 from $129,582. During this period, the median wealth of the upper-income tier was essentially unchanged—it rose by 1%, to $574,788 from $569,905. Meantime, the wealth of the lower-income tier plunged by 45%, albeit from a much smaller base, to $10,151 from $18,421."; *The Rise ofResidential Segregation by Income,* by Richard Fry and Paul Taylor, http://www.pewsocialtrends.org /2012/08/01/the-rise-of-residential-segregation-by-income/, in part, "Residential segregation by income has increased during the past three decades across the United States and in 27 of the nation's 30 largest major metropolitan areas, according to a new analysis of census tract and household income data by the Pew Research Center."; *The Great Recession and Land and Housing Loss in African American Communities: Case Studies from Alabama, Florida, Louisiana, and Mississippi,* by Charlotte Otabor, M.A. and Jessica Gordan Nembhard, Ph.D., http://www.coas.howard.edu /centeronraceandwealth/reports%26publications/0512-great-recession-andland-housing-loss-in-african-american-communities-part1.pdf, in part, "According to Dillihunt et al (2010, p. vi), in 2009, a disproportionate share of the families impacted by the 3.4 million homes in foreclosure were people of color. They were "systematically targeted by the financial industry for predatory, subprime loans. In fact, over half of the mortgages to African-Americans in recent years were high-cost subprime loans, mostly to people who would have qualified for regular loans.""; Wealth Stripping: Why it Costs so Much to Be Poor, by James H. Carr, http://www.democracyjournal.org /26/wealth-stripping-why-it-costs-so-much-to-be-poor.php?page=2, in part, "The higher numbers of foreclosures among minority households related to predatory loan products has been extensively documented.

Prince George's County in Maryland is the highest-income majority African-American county in the nation and, ironically, also the foreclosure capital of that state. In a recent study on foreclosures in that community, high-income borrowers in African-American neighborhoods were 42 percent more likely to go into foreclosure than typical borrowers in white neighborhoods. High-income borrowers in Latino communities fared worse: They were about 160 percent more likely to experience a foreclosure."; *Foreclosures cost communities of color $1 trillion in home equity*, by Charlene Crowell, http://www.ncpolicywatch.com/2012/10/29/foreclosures-cost-communities-ofcolor-1-trillion-in-home-equity/

End Notes for the Civil Rights Implications of Eminent Domain Abuse

[1] Panelist Professor Ilya Somin at transcript pp. 9-10.

[2] Briefing Report at page 23.

[3] Mount Holly v. Mount Holly Gardens Citizens, Inc., Supreme Court docket 11-1507, Dec. 4, 2013.

[4] This is precisely what happened in another disparate impact housing case two years ago in *Magner v. Gallagher* when the City of St. Paul, the plaintiff, dismissed its claim before the Court could hear it. It was widely reported that the U.S. Department of Justice intervened and convinced St. Paul to settle before trial.

[5] See http://blog.nj.com/njv_guest_blog/2013/11/the_feds_are_running_from_a_ne.html and http://www.reuters.com/article/2013/10/31/usa-court-discrimination-idUSL1N0IL24L20131031 and http://www.philly.com/philly/news/local/20131101 Tentative settlement in Mount Holly Gardens case.html.

End Notes for U.S. Commission on Civil Rights Statement for "The Civil Rights Implications of Eminent Domain Abuse" Commissioner Roberta Achtenberg

[1] This comment is not to be interpreted as criticism of the Commission staff who developed the record and created the Report. Such data, in fact, may not exist. *See, e.g.,* United States Government Accountability Office, *Eminent Domain: Information About Its Uses and Effect on Property Owners and Communities is Limited*, GAO-07-28, November 2006, *available at* http://www.gao.gov/new.items/d0728.pdf.

[2] Kladney, Dave, *Statement on Eminent Domain*, November 2013, appended to this Report.

[3] United States Commission on Civil Rights, *Briefing Transcript*, August 12, 2011, p. 83, l. 10, *available at* http://www.usccr.gov/calendar/trnscrpt/08-12-11ccr1.pdf: COMMISSIONER ACHTENBERG: I want to direct this question to Professor Byrne, if I might. My concern in reading the materials has been that the data, at least as far as I can tell, is questionable in terms of the statistics that are available to us about what has happened, let's say, since 1980 or 1990 or in the most recent decade past in terms of the allegations that it is clearly a disparate impact that is being felt as a result of eminent domain on minorities and other

disempowered communities. I'm wondering, am I missing something or is the data as scanty as our current record makes it appear?

MR. BYRNE: I think there is a big problem with a lack of empirical study of the employment of eminent domain, certainly, as you say, in the last two decades or so, done to rigorous social science standards. We really don't know very much about the incidence and who is affected by it. And so I think that would be an enormous benefit and I think something that is agreed across the political spectrum that a better understanding of what actually occurs would be helpful.

[4] *See, e.g.,* United States Commission on Civil Rights, *The Civil Rights Implications ofEminent Domain Abuse*, 2013, p. 11 and p. 38; and Kelly, James J., *"We Shall Not Be Moved": Urban Communities, Eminent Domain and the Socioeconomics of Just Compensation*, St. John's L. Rev 923, p. 80 (Notre Dame Law School Scholarly Works, Paper 833, January 1, 2006), *available at* http://scholarship.law.nd.edu/cgi/viewcontent.cgi? article=1820& context=law faculty scholarship&seiredir=1&referer=http%3A%2F%2 Fwww.google.com %2Furl%3Fsa%3Dt%26rct%3Dj%26q%3Deminent%2520domain%2520tenant%2520 rights%2520law%2520review%26source%3Dweb%26cd%3D116%26ved%3D0CEcQFjAF OG4%26url%3D http%253A%252F%252Fscholarship.law.nd.edu%252Fcgi%252Fviewcontent.cgi%253 Farticle%253D1820%2526context%253Dlaw_faculty_scholarship%26ei%3DfX1-UvbMNPXFsAScsID4Bw%26usg%3DAFQjCNGXsJWmAttbv4iTIc2QUwaCDg3yag%26 sig2%3DKyvOfGpXfImbOL59N EihYA#search=%22eminent%20domain%20tenant%20 rights%20law%20review%22.

[5] *See, e.g.,* United States Commission on Civil Rights, *The Civil Rights Implications ofEminent Domain Abuse*, 2013, pp. 11 - 13 and p. 18.

End Notes for Statement and Rebuttal of Commissioner Gail Heriot

[1] Chairman Castro also suggests that the Commission instead ought to be more concerned with the disproportionate effects of the mortgage crisis on racial and ethnic minorities. Draft Castro Statement at 1. In 2009, the topic of the Commission's annual enforcement report was "Civil Rights and the Mortgage Crisis." It addresses these issues at some length.

[2] I was also surprised to read in my colleague Commissioner Kladney's statement that he understood some of the conservative commissioners and libertarian panelists to be in favor of a national standard on eminent domain, in contrast to their preference for decentralization in other areas of public policy. The Fifth Amendment, of course, already sets forth a national standard regarding takings. But I did not understand any of the panelists or my colleagues to be in favor of national legislation on this issue. Indeed, I share my colleague Commissioner Gaziano's concerns about adopting proposed recommendations that would ask the Department of Justice to develop a uniform standard for just compensation. I do not favor federal legislation imposing uniform standards that goes beyond what I believe the Constitution already requires.

[3] Some sections of the testimony presented in this report contain information that I found illuminating on these questions. See, for example, my exchange with Professor Ilya Somin on alternative methods for alleviating "blight" summarized at 21. On the viability of "secret assembly" by private developers as an alternative to eminent domain for large-scale

development exchanges, see the discussion between Professor Somin and Commissioner Yaki summarized at 22-23.

[4] For another example of a report where the Commission has investigated the racially adverse effects of a public policy that may seem counter-intuitive to some people, see U.S. Commission on Civil Rights, *The Impact ofIllegal Immigration on the Wages and Employment Opportunities ofBlack Workers* (2010) (panelists and Commissioners debated empirical literature on whether current enforcement of immigration policy has an adverse effect on the wages and employment opportunities of African-American workers).

[5] See, e.g., Goodwin Liu, *Roberts Would Swing the Supreme Court to the Right*, BLOOMBERG, July 22, 2005 ("Before becoming a judge, [then Supreme Court nominee John Roberts] belonged to the Republican National Lawyers' Association and the National Legal Center for the Public Interest, whose mission is to promote (among other things) 'free enterprise,' 'private ownership of property,' and 'limited government.' These are code words for an ideological agenda hostile to environmental, workplace, and consumer protections."). Similarly, the National Lawyers Guild declares that it seeks "to unite the lawyers, law students, legal workers and jailhouse lawyers to function as an effective force ... to the end that human rights shall be regarded as more sacred than property rights." See The National Lawyers Guild: From Roosevelt through Reagan (Ann Fagan Ginger & Eugene M. Tobin, eds. 1988). The slogan fails to acknowledge that property rights *are* human rights. See also James W. Ely Jr., *Colloquium, Reflections on* Buchanan v. Warley, *Private Property, and Race*, 51 VAND. L. REV. 953, 954 (May 1998): "The landmark decision of *Buchanan v. Warley* has long deserved greater attention from scholars.... One can only speculate about the lack of scholarly interest in *Buchanan*. Possibly, the dual nature of *Buchanan* has made it difficult for scholars to assess. Perhaps the property-centered focus of Buchanan made the case awkward for post-New Deal liberals, who are indifferent at best to the constitutional protection of property rights. Clearly *Buchanan* does not fit neatly into post-New Deal jurisprudence, with its artificial and unhistorical division between the rights of property owners and other individual liberties. Such factors may have caused scholars to overlook or intentionally downplay *Buchanan*."

[6] Frederick Douglass, *Comments on Gerrit Smith's Address*, in FREDERICK DOUGLASS: SELECTED SPEECHES AND WRITINGS (Philip S. Foner and Yuval Taylor, eds. 2000).

[7] See written testimony of Professor Ilya Somin at 27.

[8] See Wendell Pritchett, *The "Public Menace" ofBlight: Urban Renewal and the Private Use ofEminent Domain*, 20 YALE L. & POL'Y REV. 1, 7-8 (2003): "To secure political and judicial approval for their efforts, renewal advocates created a new language of urban decline: a discourse of blight. Blight, renewal proponents argued, was a disease that threatened to turn healthy areas into slums. A vague, amorphous term, blight was a rhetorical device that enabled renewal advocates to reorganize property ownership by declaring certain real estate dangerous to the future of the city. To make the case for renewal programs, advocates contrasted the existing, deteriorated state of urban areas with the modern, efficient city that would replace them. Urban revitalization required the condemnation of blighted properties and the transfer of this real estate to developers who would use it more productively...."

Also: "The role of blight terminology in restricting racial mobility has also been under-appreciated by legal scholars. Blight was a facially neutral term infused with racial and ethnic prejudice. While it purportedly assessed the state of urban infrastructure, blight was often used to describe the negative impact of certain residents on city neighborhoods. This 'scientific' method of understanding urban decline was used to justify the removal of blacks and other minorities from certain parts of the city. By selecting racially changing neighborhoods as blighted areas and designating them for redevelopment, the urban renewal program enabled institutional and political elites to relocate minority populations and entrench racial segregation." *Id.* at 18.

Also: "In periods of migration, these areas were 'invaded' by ethnic and racial minorities in search of affordable housing. This use of medical terminology by the Chicago school made its analysis appear objective and scientific, but it also reflected the general prejudices of society regarding racial minorities, particularly blacks. In his discussion of Chicago, Burgess noted the 'disturbances of metabolism caused by an excessive increase [in population] such as those which followed the great influx of southern Negroes' into the city after World War I. These waves of people caused a 'speeding up of the junking process in the area of deterioration.' Another study, which acknowledged that many areas occupied by blacks had other unattractive features, concluded that 'certain racial and national groups ... cause a greater physical deterioration of property than groups higher in the social and economic scale.' Blight, therefore, may have been a naturally occurring process, but racial minorities were central to the Chicago school's understanding of urban change." Id.

[9] *Id.* at 1.

[10] *Id.* at 41.

[11] Report at 5, citing Brief for Nat'l Ass'n for the Advancement of Colored People et al. as Amici Curiae Supporting Petitioners at 7, in Kelo v. New London, 545 U.S. 469 (2005) (No. 04-108), *available at* http://www.ij.org/ images/pdf_folder/private_property/kelo/naacp02.pdf.

[12] *Housing Project Hangs Fire: Charges 'Clearance' ofNegroes is Aim*, CHI. DEFENDER, May 7, 1949, at 4 (quoted in Pritchett, *supra* note 6, at 35).

[13] Quoted in Pritchett, *supra* note 8, at 33.

[14] *See* Mindy Thompson Fullilove, EMINENT DOMAIN AND AFRICAN AMERICANS: WHAT IS THE PRICE OF THE COMMONS? (2007).

[15] *Id.* at 2.

[16] 545 U.S. 469 (2005).

[17] See, e.g., The Institute for Justice, *Victimizing the Vulnerable* (2007) (finding that properties targeted for takings are disproportionately likely to be found in low-income or disproportionately minority neighborhoods). This study looks only at the census tract where takings took place and not at data on the demographics of the owners themselves. Although I would welcome research that could better pinpoint the race and income level of the targeted property owners themselves, alas, to my knowledge, it does not yet exist.

In the copy of his Draft Statement provided to me, Commissioner Kladney states that "Despite my requests during the briefing for data about recent instances of eminent domain abuse that fall within our jurisdiction, none of the witnesses pointed to cases after 1973. Only after they revised their statements for the record were any of the witnesses able to point to relevant cases after 1973." Commissioner Kladney's actual question to the witnesses was: "Have any of these types of cases shown a violation of civil rights or property rights, like *Kelo* and *Hawaiian Housing Authority* and things like that, or have they withstood these court tests, constitutionality?" Transcript at 77-78. Ilya Somin, the only witness who responded, described a series of cases involving takings dubiously constitutional even under what Somin believes to be the overly permissive *Kelo* standard of review. He appears not to have understood Commissioner Kladney to be asking for a list of cases involving allegations of intentional racial discrimination, and I interpret the language that appears in the official transcript in the same way.

I am also somewhat confused about the claim that witnesses found cases after 1973 only after the briefing was over, as none revised or resubmitted new statements. I would note also that the Institute for Justice website cites plenty of cases of post-1973 litigation involving eminent domain abuse.

[18] A tangential but nonetheless important point: Professor Byrne said that that in his view eminent domain abuse has improved in recent years in part due to lessened federal involvement and increased local control over housing and urban policy. Report at 10. Often, my Democratic colleagues on the Commission have assumed that increasing federal control over a given area of public policy will automatically redound to the benefit of historically disadvantaged groups. Equally often, I have pushed back against such claims. See, e.g., U.S. Commission on Civil Rights, *Peer to Peer Violence and Bullying: Measuring the Federal Response* (2011), Statement of Gail Heriot at 196: "What disturbs me is the lack of real discussion in [my colleagues'] Statements. Nowhere is an effort made to explain how federal jurisdiction over these things is making the issue better. The point is taken for granted. The Statements contain no recognition of the fact that entrusting an issue—especially an important issue—to the federal bureaucracy has costs." I hope that Professor Byrne's comments prompt all of us to examine critically the all too common assumption that federalization always benefits minorities. Often, as here, the picture is not so simple.

[19] One of the findings and recommendations that Chairman Castro proposed to the Commission suggested that homeowners should be provided greater compensation than owners of businesses. As I discuss in the text above, I agree that protecting the rights of homeowners is important. At the same time, owners of businesses may be equally or more vulnerable to the ill effects of takings for somewhat different reasons. Some neighborhood businesses rely heavily on customer goodwill that has been built up for a number of years. A restaurant might be beloved in the neighborhood where it has been located for 20 years, but might struggle to attract new customers two miles away on a different side of town. This kind of injury is not ordinarily compensated for when a government exercises eminent domain.

[20] Shelton Statement at 41.

[21] Interestingly, Mindy Thompson Fullilove has even argued that urban renewal and the displacement of African-American urban neighborhood culture led to the decline ofjazz at mid-century. EMINENT DOMAIN AND AFRICAN-AMERICANS: WHAT IS THE PRICE OF THE COMMONS? at 6.

[22] But setting in place too many additional procedures can make it harder for property owners to challenge the system, especially the poorest and the least educated who often have the most difficulty navigating complex legal procedures and/or affording lawyers who can help them do so.

[23] Dana Berliner, *Opening the Floodgates*, Institute for Justice, 2006 (the number of private condemnations threatened or undertaken in the year after *Kelo* was about half of the total number undertaken in the five years from 1998 through 2002). I am not aware of any empirical studies that have come to a different conclusion.

[24] In such spare time as the Commission affords me, I enjoy studying the history of department stores, and I am therefore partial to a formulation of the point made during the debate over eminent domain abuse in New York in the 1950s: "Faced with a clear crisis in cities, only a few policy-makers expressed concerns about the possible abuse of eminent domain powers. New York housing reformer Charles Abrams was one. 'In my opinion, under present redevelopment laws, Macy's could condemn Gimbels - if Robert Moses gave the word,' Abrams argued." Pritchett, *supra* at note 8, at 37.

[25] U.S. Supreme Court Oral Argument Transcript, Kelo v. City of New London, 04-108 (argued Feb. 22, 2005), at 21.

[26] Ilya Somin, *Controlling the Grasping Hand: Economic Development After Kelo*, 15 SUP. CT. ECON. REV. 183, 195-6 (2007). It is difficult to tell whether the number ofjobs created outweighed the jobs lost by displacing Poletown's former residents and businesses. For a fuller discussion of the limited figures available about the likely results of these condemnations, see Somin at 197-98.

[27] Testimony of Susette Kelo, Lead Plaintiff, Kelo v. City of New London, Before the Committee on the Judiciary Subcommittee on the Constitution and Civil Justice, U.S. House of Representatives, Hearing on Private Property Rights Protection Act of 2013 (Apr. 18, 2013).

[28] See *Statement of Gail Heriot* in U.S. Commission on Civil Rights, *School Discipline and Disparate Impact* (2012) (tough school discipline policies may have the benefit of ensuring classroom order, which can be particularly important in often-chaotic inner city schools—even if those policies have an unintended disparate impact).

End Notes for Statement on Eminent Domain

[1] 42 USC 1975a(a).

[2] Beyond attention to these issues, the Commission is also concerned with voting fraud. See: 42 USC § 1975.

[3] USCCR Briefing Transcript, Aug. 11, 2011 ("Briefing Transcript") Testimony of Professor Byrne at 25. See also, Id at 84 (describing the imprecision of the data used in Victimizing the Vulnerable).

[4] Briefing Statement of David Beito at 5 ("McCall suspects that wealthy developers are trying to get their hands on the property.")

[5] Ibid. pp. 40-41.

[6] Ibid. p. 42.

[7] When the USCCR held immigration briefing in Birmingham, AL one year after our eminent domain briefing, I asked Mr. Beito what the outcome of these two anecdotal cases were...he did not know at that time.

[8] Ibid. p. 76.

[9] Somin at page 31. Shelton at page 40. Beito, whose cases were cited during the briefing, at pages 44-46.

[10] See Somin written testimony, in the Commission's Report page 31. In the written statement, Beito references the two cases that he discussed in the briefing (see report, pp.44-45).

[11] Mindy Thompson Fullilove, *Root Shock: How Tearing Up City Neighborhoods Hurts America, and What We Can Do About It*, p. 17. Mindy Fullilove is a medical doctor, whose authority to write of the issue of eminent domain is based on her personal experiences rather than formal training on the issue. Derek Werner, Note: The Public Use Clause, Common Sense and Takings, 10 B. U. Pub. Int. L. J., 335 (2001). Bernard J. Frieden & Lynn B. Sagalyn, *Downtown, Inc.: How America Rebuilds Cities*, p. 29.

[12] Professor Byrne cited an instance of eminent domain in Washington, D.C. but stated that it was necessary for the construction of "a badly needed private supermarket for an underserved community." Transcript pp. 22-23.

[13] These Clark County casinos and hotels where first envisioned in 1946, with the opening of the Flamingo Hotel— which is more than five miles away from the downtown area.

[14] Scott J. Kennelly, In Honor of Walter O. Weyrach: Florida's Eminent Domain Overhaul: Creating More Problems than it Solved, 60 Fla. L. Rev. 471 (2008) Available at: http://scholarship.law.ufl.edu/flr/vol60/iss2/5.

End Notes for Panelists' Written Statements

[1] BARACK OBAMA, THE AUDACITY OF HOPE 149 (2006).

[2] *See, e.g.,* JENNIFER NEDELSKY, PRIVATE PROPERTY AND THE LIMITS OF AMERICAN CONSTITUTIONALISM: THE MADISONIAN FRAMEWORK AND ITS LEGACY (1990) (emphasizing centrality of property rights for the Founders); JAMES W. ELY, JR., THE GUARDIAN OF EVERY OTHER RIGHT: A CONSTITUTIONAL HISTORY OF PROPERTY RIGHTS 42-58 (3d. ed. 2008) (emphasizing centrality of property rights for the Founding generation); Stuart Bruchey, *The Impact of Concern for the Security ofProperty Rights on the Legal System of the Early American Republic*, 1980 WIS. L. REV. 1135, 1136 (noting that "[p]erhaps the most important value of the Founding Fathers of the American constitutional period, 'was their belief in the necessity of securing property rights'").

[3] I have summarized the second class status of property rights in current Supreme Court jurisprudence in Ilya Somin, *Taking Property Rights Seriously? The Supreme Court and the "Poor Relation" of Constitutional Law,* George Mason Univ. Law & Econ. Res. Paper No. 08-53 (2008), *available at* http://papers.ssrn.com/sol3/papers.cfm?abstract id=1247854.

[4] 545 U.S. 469 (2005).

[5] U.S. Const. Amend. V.

[6] *Kelo v. City ofNew London*, 545 U.S. 469, 473-78 (2005).

[7] *See Hawaii Housing Auth. v. Midkiff* , 467 U.S. 229, 241 (1984) (ruling that takings are for a public use if they are "rationally related to a conceivable public purpose"); *Berman v. Parker*, 348 U.S. 26, 32 (1954) (holding that the legislature has "well-nigh conclusive" power to define public use as it sees fit).

[8] *Berman*, 348 U.S. at 32.

[9] *Midkiff*, 467 U.S. at 240-41.

[10] *See* James W. Ely, Jr., *"Poor Relation" Once More: The Supreme Court and the Vanishing Rights ofProperty Owners,* 2005 CATO SUP. CT. REV. 39, 40-43 (describing early American jurists' rejection of the idea that eminent domain can be used to transfer property from one private party to another without giving the general public any right to use it). *See also* Eric R. Claeys, *Public Use Limitations and Natural Property Rights,* 2004 MICH .ST. L. REV. 877, 894-905 (2004) (symposium issue) (detailed discussion of limited eighteenth and nineteenth century conceptions of public use that banned most private-toprivate takings).

[11] *Id.* at 62.

[12] AKHIL REED AMAR, THE BILL OF RIGHTS: CREATION AND RECONSTRUCTION 268-69 (1998).

[13] On the centrality of property rights in nineteenth century conceptions of civil rights, see, e.g., HAROLD HYMAN & WILLIAM WIECEK, EQUAL JUSTICE UNDER LAW: CONSTITUTIONAL DEVELOPMENT, 1835-75 395-97 (1982) (describing the right to

property as one of the main elements of civil rights as conceived in the 1860s, along with the right to contract, the right to marry, and the right of access to the courts); MARK A. GRABER, TRANSFORMING FREE SPEECH: THE AMBIGUOUS LEGACY OF CIVIL LIBERTARIANISM (1991) (describing how most nineteenth century jurists viewed property as a fundamental civil right).

[14] *Kelo*, 545 U.S. at 477-78.

[15] For a discussion of the relevant cases, see Ilya Somin, *The Judicial Reaction to* Kelo, 4 ALBANY GOVT. L. REV. 1 25-35 (2011) (Introduction to Symposium on Eminent Domain in the United States).

[16] *Kelo*, 545 U.S. at 469-78.

[17] *Id.* at 487-89 (rejecting property owners' argument that the government must prove a "reasonable certainty" that the development project will succeed, and refusing to "second-guess the City's considered judgments about the efficacy of its development plan").

[18] Somin, *Judicial Reaction* at 34-35.

[19] *See City ofNorwood v. Horney*, 853 N.E.2d 1115, 1141 (Ohio 2006) (holding that "economic development" alone does not justify condemnation); *Bd. of Cnty. Comm'rs ofMuskogee Cnty. v. Lowery*, 136 P.3d 639, 653-54 (Okla. 2006) (holding that "economic development" is not a "public purpose" under the Oklahoma State Constitution, and rejecting *Kelo* as a guide to interpretation of Oklahoma's state Public Use Clause); *Benson v. State*, 710 N.W.2d 131, 146 (S.D. 2006) (concluding that the South Dakota Constitution gives property owners broader protection than *Kelo* and requires "actual use" of the condemned property by the government or the public); *County of Wayne v. Hathcock*, 684 NW2d 765 (Mich. 2004) (rejecting "economic development" rationale for condemnation); *Sw. Ill. Dev. Auth. v. Nat'l City Envtl., L.L.C.*, 768 N.E.2d 1, 9, 11 (Ill. 2002) (holding that a "contribu[tion] to positive economic growth in the region" is not a public use justifying condemnation); *Cnty. of Wayne v. Hathcock*, 684 N.W.2d 765, 770, 778 (Mich. 2004) (invalidating economic development takings under the Michigan Constitution*); City ofBozeman v. Vaniman*, 898 P.2d 1208, 1214 (Mont. 1995) (holding that a condemnation that transfers property to a private business is unconstitutional unless the transfer to the business is insignificant and incidental to a public project); *Ga. Dep't of Transp. v. Jasper Cnty.*, 586 S.E.2d 853, 856 (S.C. 2003) (holding that even a substantial "projected economic benefit. . . cannot justify a condemnation."); *Baycol, Inc v Downtown Development Authority*, 315 So. 2d 451, 457 (Fla. 1975) (holding that a "'public [economic] benefit' is not synonymous with 'public purpose' as a predicate which can justify eminent domain"); *In re Petition of Seattle*, 638 P.2d 549, 556-57 (Wash 1981) (disallowing plan to use eminent domain to build retail shopping, where purpose was not elimination of blight); *Owensboro v McCormick*, 581 SW2d 3, 8 (Ky. 1979) ("No 'public use' is involved where the land of A is condemned merely to enable B to build a factory"); *Karesh v City of Charleston*, 247 S.E. 2d 342, 345 (S.C. 1978) (striking down taking justified only by economic development); *City ofLittle Rock v Raines*, 411 S.W. 2d 486, 495 (Ark. 1967) (private economic development project not a public use); *Hogue v Port of Seattle*, 341 P.2d 171, 181-191 (Wash. 1959) (denying condemnation of residential property so that agency could "devote it to what it considers a higher and better economic use,"); *Opinion of the Justices*, 131 A. 2d 904, 905-06 (Me. 1957) (condemnation for industrial development to enhance economy not a public use); *City ofBozeman v Vaniman*, 898 P2d 1208, 1214-15 (Mont. 1995) (holding that a condemnation that transfers property to a "private business" is unconstitutional unless the transfer to the business is "insignificant" and "incidental" to a public project).

[20] See discussion in Part III, *infra.*

[21] For a discussion of the reasons for this pattern see Ilya Somin, *Controlling the Grasping Hand: Economic Development Takings After* Kelo, 15 SUP. CT. ECON. REV. 183, 190-203 (2007).

[22] *See generally* Wendell Pritchett, *The "Public Menace" ofBlight: Urban Renewal and the Private Uses ofEminent Domain*, 21 YALE L. & POL'Y REV. 1 (2003) (describing origins of these laws); Ilya Somin, *Blight,* ENCYCLOPEDIA OF HOUSING (forthcoming) (same); Amy Lavine, *From Slum Clearance To Economic Development: A Retrospective of Redevelopment Policies in New York State* 4 ALB. GOVT. L. REV. 212 (2011) (describing origins of New York's important early blight laws).

[23] Somin, *Grasping Hand* at 269-71.

[24] *Id.* For studies documenting the disproportionate impact of blight and urban renewal takings on minorities, see MARTIN ANDERSON, THE FEDERAL BULLDOZER 64-65 (1965); MINDY THOMPSON FULLILOVE, ROOT SHOCK: HOW TEARING CITY NEIGHBORHOODS HURTS AMERICA, AND WHAT WE CAN DO ABOUT IT ch. 4 (2004); Benjamin B. Quinones, *Redevelopment Redefined: Revitalizing the Central City with Resident Control,* 27 U. MICH. J. L. & REFORM, 680, 740-41 (1994) (same); Pritchett, *The "Public Menace" ofBlight*; Mindy Thompson Fullilove, *Eminent Domain and African-Americans* (Institute for Justice, 2007).

[25] Pritchett, *The "Public Menace" ofBlight*, at 47; FULLILOVE, ROOT SHOCK ch. 4. James Baldwin famously stated that "urban renewal ... means moving the Negroes out. It means Negro removal, that is what it means." Citizen King: Three Perspectives, PBS Transcript, available at http://www.pbs.org/wgbh/amex/mlk/sfeature/sf_video_pop_04_tr_qry.html.

[26] Anderson, FEDERAL BULLDOZER at 65.

[27] Fullilove, *African-Americans and Eminent Domain*, at 2.

[28] Somin, *Grasping Hand*, at 269-71.

[29] Anderson, FEDERAL BULLDOZER at 64-65.

[30] BERNARD FRIEDEN & LYNN SAGALYN, DOWNTOWN, INC.: HOW AMERICA REBUILDS CITIES 28-29 (1989) (noting role of "racism" in urban renewal and highway takings); Pritchett, *Public Menace*; at Herbert J. Gans, *The Failure of Urban Renewal*, in URBAN RENEWAL: THE RECORD AND THE CONTROVERSY, 539 (ed. James Q. Wilson, 1966) (noting that "the urban renewal program has often been characterized as Negro clearance, and in too many cities, this has been its intent.").

[31] Quoted in FRIEDEN & SAGALYN, DOWNTOWN at 28.

[32] Somin, *Grasping Hand*, at 269-71.

[33] 348 U.S. 26 (1954).

[34] *Id.* at 36.

[35] *Id.*

[36] HOWARD GILLETTE, JR., BETWEEN JUSTICE AND BEAUTY: RACE, PLANNING, AND THE FAILURE OF URBAN POLICY IN WASHINGTON, D.C. 163-64 (1995).

[37] Pritchett, *"Public Menace" ofBlight* at 47.

[38] *Id.* at 47.

[39] *See* Ilya Somin, *Let there Be Blight: Blight Condemnations in New York after* Goldstein *and* Kaur, FORDHAM URB. L. J. (forthcoming) (symposium on Eminent Domain in New York); Lavine, *From Slum Clearance To Economic Development.*

[40] *See* Ilya Somin, *Blight Sweet Blight*, LEGAL TIMES, Aug. 14, 2006, at 42; Colin Gordon, *Blighting the Way: Urban Renewal, Economic Development, and the Elusive Definition ofBlight*, 31 FORDHAM URB. L.J. 305, 307 (2004).

[41] *See City ofLas Vegas Downtown Redev. Agency v. Pappas,* 76 P.3d 1, 12-15 (Nev. 2003) (holding that downtown Las Vegas is blighted); and *In re W. 41st St. Realty v. N.Y. State Urban Dev. Corp.*, 744 N.Y.S.2d 121 (N.Y. App. Div. 2002) (holding that Times Square is blighted).

[42] *See Matter ofKaur v. N.Y. State Urban Dev. Corp.*, 933 N.E.2d 721 (N.Y. 2010); and *Matter of Goldstein v. N.Y. State Urban Dev. Corp.,* 921 N.E.2d 164 (N.Y. 2009). For a detailed discussion of these two cases and the abuses involved, see Somin, *Let There be Blight.* Among the abuses overlooked by the New York Court of Appeals were that the firm conducting the "blight" study on behalf of the condemning authority was on the payroll of the private interests who would receive the condemned property, and the fact that those same interests may have been responsible for much of the "blight" in question. *Id.*

[43] *See Kelo*, 545 U.S. at 475 (noting that "[t]here is no allegation that any of these properties [that were condemned] is blighted or otherwise in poor condition").

[44] *See* Somin, *Grasping Hand* at 190-203, 267-69 (detailing these dangers).

[45] *See, e.g.,* DICK CARPENTER & JOHN ROSS, EMPIRE STATE EMINENT DOMAIN: ROBIN HOOD IN REVERSE (2010), available at http://www.ij.org/about/3045 (describing extensive use of eminent domain in New York, especially against poor and minority neighborhoods); Dick Carpenter & John Ross, *Testing O'Connor And Thomas: Does The Use OfEminent Domain Target Poor And Minority Communities?* 46 URBAN STUD. 2447 (2009).

[46] *See* Brief for the National Ass'n for the Advancement of Colored People et al. as Amici Curiae Supporting Petitioners, *Kelo*, 545 U.S. 469 (2004) (No. 04 - 108), 2004 WL 2811057.

[47] *Id.* at 7-12.

[48] *Matter ofKaur v. N.Y. State Urban Dev. Corp.,* 933 N.E.2d 721 (N.Y. 2010).

[49] *See* Somin, *Let There Be Blight* (describing the details of this case and its background).

[50] Somin, *Grasping Hand* at 192-99.

[51] JEFF BENEDICT, LITTLE PINK HOUSE: A TRUE STORY OF DEFIANCE AND COURAGE 377-78 (2009); Ilya Somin, *Stronger Protections Needed,* N.Y. TIMES ROOM FOR DEBATE BLOG: A TURNING POINT FOR EMINENT DOMAIN?, Nov. 12, 2009, available at http://roomfordebate.blogs.nytimes.com/2009/11/12/a-turning-point-for-eminent-domain/#ilya.

[52] *Poletown Neighborhood Council v. City ofDetroit,* 304 N.W.2d 455, 457, 459 (Mich. 1981), *overruled by County of Wayne v. Hathcock*, 684 N.W.2d 765 (Mich. 2004).

[53] For a detailed discussion of the costs and benefits of the Poletown takings, see Ilya Somin, *Overcoming* Poletown: County of Wayne v. Hathcock, *Economic Development Takings, and the Future ofPublic Use,* 2004 MICH. ST. L. REV. 1005, 1016- 19 (2004) (symposium on *County of Wayne v. Hathcock*).

[54] *See, e.g., Kirby Forest Indus. Inc. v. United States*, 467 U.S. 1, 10 (1984).

[55] *See* Thomas Mitchell, et al., *Forced Sale Risk: Class, Race, and the "Double Discount,"* 37 FLA. ST. U. L. REV. 589, 630- 38 (2010) (citing numerous studies showing undercompensation); Yun-chien Chang, *An Empirical Study of Compensation Paid in Eminent Domain Settlements: New York City 1990-2002*, 39 J. LEGAL STUD. 201 (2010) (finding systematic undercompensation in the majority of New York City cases).

[56] *See* Chang, *An Empirical Study of Compensation.*

[57] Somin, *Grasping Hand* at 215-16.

[58] *See id.* at 190-203 (explaining why the politically weak are likely to be targeted for condemnation).

[59] CENSUS BUREAU, INCOME, POVERTY, AND HEALTH INSURANCE COVERAGE IN THE UNITED STATES: 2009 16 (Sept. 2010), available at http://www.census.gov /prod/2010pubs/p60-238.pdf.

[60] *See, e.g.,* LARRY BARTELS, UNEQUAL DEMOCRACY (2010); Martin Gilens, *Inequality and Democratic Responsiveness*, 69 PUB. OPINION Q. 778 (2005).

[61] *See generally* DONALD KINDER & CINDY KAM, US AGAINST THEM: ETHNOCENTRIC FOUNDATIONS OF AMERICAN PUBLIC OPINION (2009).

[62] *See, e.g.,* Thomas W. Merrill, *The Economics ofPublic Use*, 72 CORNELL L. REV. 61, 72-81 (1986) (describing holdout rationale for eminent domain); Lynn Blais, *Urban Revitalization in the Post-Kelo Era*, 34 FORDHAM URBAN L.J. 657 (2007) (arguing that eminent domain is needed to revitalize urban areas).

[63] For a good theoretical discussion of this problem, see Lloyd R. Cohen, *Holdouts and Free Riders*, 20 J. LEGAL STUD. 351 (1991).

[64] For more detailed discussions of these advantages of secret assembly over eminent domain, Somin, *Grasping Hand* at 203- 09, and Daniel B. Kelly, *The "Public Use" Requirement in Eminent Domain Law: A Rationale Based on Secret Purchases and Private Influence*, 92 CORNELL L. REV. 1 (2006).

[65] *See* Kelly, *The "Public Use" Requirement in Eminent Domain Law.*

[66] Ilya Somin, *The Limits ofBacklash: Assessing the Political Response to Kelo,* 93 MINN. L. REV. 2100, 2108-14 (2009).

[67] [The number of states enacting reform legislation on economic development takings increased to 44 after the Commission held its briefing, as indicated earlier in this report. -Ed.]

[68] *Id.* at 2101-02. For the most comprehensive analysis of post-Kelo reform legislation, see id. at 2114-53. See also Edward J. López et al., *Pass a Law, Any Law, State Legislative Responses to the* Kelo *Backlash*, 5 REV. LAW & ECON. 101, (2009), available at http://www.bepress.com/rle/vol5/iss1/art5/; Andrew Morriss, *Symbol or Substance? An Empirical Assessment of State Responses to* Kelo, 17 SUP. CT. ECON. REV. 237, (2009); James W. Ely, Jr., *Post-*Kelo *Reform: Is the Glass Half-Full or Half-Empty?,* 17 SUP. CT. ECON. REV. 127 (2009); Timothy Sandefur, *The "Backlash" So Far: Will Americans Get Meaningful Eminent Domain Reform?,* 2006 MICH. ST. L. REV. 709 (2006); Lynn Blais, *Urban Revitalization in the PostKelo Era*, 34 FORDHAM URBAN L.J. 657 (2007).

[69] Somin, *Limits ofBacklash*, at 2120-35.

[70] *Id.* at 2120-28. See also the discussion of blight condemnations in § II.B., *infra.*

[71] *Id.* at 2117-20.

[72] *Id.*

[73] *Id.* at 2154-70.

[74] Somin, *Blight* (forthcoming). The state of Utah banned blight condemnations even before *Kelo,* but partially rescinded the ban in 2007, allowing such takings to occur if approved by a supermajority of property owners in the affected area. Somin, *Limits ofBacklash,* at 2138 & n. 176.

[75] Testimony of David Beito, Chair of the Alabama State Advisory Commission on Civil Rights, U.S. Commission on Civil Rights, hearing on "The Civil Rights Implications of Eminent Domain Abuse," Aug. 12, 2011.

[76] *See* Steven J. Eagle, *Does Blight Really Justify Condemnation?* 39 URBAN LAWYER 833 (2007).

[77] *See* Ilya Somin, *Why Robbing Peter Won't Help Poor Paul: Low-Income Neighborhoods and Uncompensated Regulatory Takings,* 117 YALE L.J. POCKET PART 71 (2007).

End Notes

[1] 545 U.S. 469, 521-22 (2005).

[2] *See e.g.,* Marc B. Mihaly, *Living in the Past: The* Kelo *Court and Public-Private Economic Redevelopment*, 34 ECOLOGY L. Q. 1 (2007); Robert G. Dreher and John D. Echeverria, "*Kelo's* Unanswered Questions: The Policy Debate Over the Use of Eminent Domain for Economic Development," 2006, at http://www.law.georgetown.edu/gelpi/current research/documents/GELPIReport Kelo.pdf; J. Peter Byrne, *Condemnation of Low Income Residential Communities Under the Takings Clause*, 23 U.C.L.A. J. ENVTL. L. & POL. 131 (2005); Jeff Finkle, "Eminent Domain and Economic Development," at http://law.case.edu/centers/business law/eminent domain/pdfs/Finkle eminent domain pwrpt.pdf.

[3] 348 U.S. 26 (1954).

[4] *See, e.g.,* Duk Hea Oh v. NCRC, 7 A. 3d 997 (D.C. 2010); Franco v. District of Columbia, 3 A.3d 300 (D.C. 2010); Rumber v. District of Columbia and NCRC, 487 F.3d 941 (D.C. Cir. 2007); Franco v. National Capital Revitalization Comm'n, 930 A.2d 160 (D.C. 2007).

[5] *See* Elizabeth A. Taylor, *The Dudley Street Neighborhood Initiative and the Power ofEminent Domain*, 36 B.C.L. Rev. 1061 (1995).

[6] DICK M. CARPENTER & JOHN K. ROSS, INSTITUTE FOR JUSTICE, VICTIMIZING THE VULNERABLE: THE DEMOGRAPHICS OF EMINENT DOMAIN ABUSE 7 (June 2007).

[7] Edward A. Imperatore, *Discriminatory Condemnations and the Fair Housing Act*, 96 GEO. L.J. 1027 (2008).

End Notes for Hilary O. Shelton, Director, NAACP Washington Bureau & Senior Vice-President for Advocacy and Policy

[1] David Bieto and Ilya Somin, *Battle Over Eminent Domain is Another Civil Rights Issue*, THE KANSAS CITY STAR, Apr. 27, 2007.

[2] Mindy Fullilove, *What is the Price of the Commons?* February 2007.

[3] Mindy Thompson Fullilove, *Root Shock: How Tearing Up City Neighborhoods Hurts America, and What We Can Do About It*, p. 17.

[4] Derek Werner, Note: The Public Use Clause, Common Sense and Takings, 10 B. U. Pub. Int. L. J., 335 (2001).

[5] Bernard J. Frieden & Lynn B. Sagalyn, *Downtown, Inc.: How America Rebuilds Cities*, p. 29.

[6] Herbert J. Gans, *The Urban Villagers: Group and Class in the life ofItalian Americans*, p. 380.

End Notes for David Beito, Chair, U.S. Commission on Civil Rights' Alabama State Advisory Committee

[1] Margaret Brown, Farella Robinson, Shana Kluck, Christina Walsh, and Don Casey provided information which was extremely helpful in the preparation of this paper. Any errors, however, are those of the author.

[2] Paul D. Moreno, *Black Americans and Organized Labor: A New History* (Baton Rouge: Louisiana University Press, 2006), 12-14; David E. Bernstein, "Philip Sober Controlling Philip Drunk: Buchanan v. Warley in Historical Perspective," VANDERBILT LAW REVIEW 51 (May 1998), 839-47; Frederick Douglass, "Comments on Gerrit Smith's Address," *The North Star,* Mar. 30, 1849, http://www.lib.rochester.edu /index.cfm?PAGE=4383, accessed July 20, 2011; Frederick Douglass, "Oration Delivered in Corinthian Hall, Rochester," July 5, 1852, http://www.lib.rochester.edu/index. cfm?PAGE=2945, accessed July 20, 2011; and Frederick Douglass to Henry C. Wright, *The Liberator,* Jan. 29 1847; reprinted in Philip Foner, ed., *Life and Writings ofFrederick Douglass,* vol. 1 (New York: International Publishers, 1950), p. 199, http://docsouth.unc.edu/neh/douglass/support9.html, accessed July 21, 2011.

[3] "Alabama Limits Eminent Domain," *Washington Times,* Aug. 4, 2005, http://www.washingtontimes.com/news/2005/aug/04/ 20050804-120711-4571r/, accessed July 20, 2011; and Ilya Somin, "Controlling the Grasping Hand: Economic Development Takings after *Kelo*," SUPREME COURT ECONOMIC REVIEW 15 (2007), 245-47.

[4] Meeting Transcript, Alabama Advisory Committee to the United States Commission on Civil Rights, Apr.29, 2008, 260- 270, copy available from the U.S. Commission on Civil Rights.

[5] Code of Alabama, 1975, 11 53-B1, http://alisondb.legislature.state.al.us/acas/CodeofAlabama /1975/coatoc.htm, accessed July 20, 2011.

[6] Radley Balko, "Blight Flight: Why is the City of Montgomery Condemning the Property of African Americans along a Civil Rights Trail?" *Slate,* Sept. 17, 2010, http://www.slate.com/id/2267743/, accessed July 20, 2011.

[7] Balko; Sarah Netter, "Montgomery Residents Accuse City of Demolishing Homes to Sidestep Eminent Domain Laws," *ABC News,* August 26, 2010, http://abcnews.go.com/US /montgomery-residents-accuse-city-demolishing-homes-sidestep-eminent/story?id=11470620 &page=2, accessed July 20, 2011; Brandon Pizzola, Maffucci Fellow at the Institute for Justice, "Authorized Demolitions Since 2010," copy in author's possession; Meeting Transcript, Alabama Advisory Committee to the United States Commission on Civil Rights, Apr. 29, 2009, 22-35, copy available from the U.S. Commission on Civil Rights.

[8] Balko; Netter; and Benjamin Solomon, "How to Steal Land in Montgomery," *False Magazine,* January 2008, http://falsemagazine. org/content/montgomery_al.php, accessed July 20, 2011.

[9] Balko; Netter; and Solomon.

[10] Balko; Netter; and Solomon.

[11] Balko; Netter; and Karen Jones to Mayor Todd Strange, Apr. 15, 2010, copy in possession of the author; Forie Jones, Certificate of Death, Dec. 21, 1989, Alabama, Center for Health Statistics.

[12] Montgomery County, Alabama, Online Property Detail Information, Owner Name: Jones Forie, C/O Matthew Jones, Parcel Number: 11-06-23-01-020-022.000, Date Extracted: June 8, 2011, copy in possession of the author; and "Eminent Domain Through the Backdoor in Montgomery," (2010) http://www.castlecoalition.org/castlewatch/3508-eminent-domain-through-the-backdoor-in-montgomery, accessed July 21, 2011.

In reply to a letter from Farella Robinson, the Regional Director of the Central Region of the U.S. Commission on Civil Rights to Mayor Todd Strange, Kimberly O. Fehl, Montgomery's City Attorney, wrote that Jones and McCall "were not identified as owners of the property in which they claim their due process was denied. The records from the office of the Montgomery County Probate Court indicate that the property owner on the

McCall property as Hannah McCall and on the Jones property as Forie Jones, c/o Matthew Jones." Fehl to Robinson, June 23, 2010, copy in possession of the author. As already mentioned, Forie and Matthew Jones both died more than a decade ago. Hannah McCall is Jimmie McCall's wife, and they are not estranged or at odds on this issue.

[13] The author would like to thank Don Casey for some of these suggestions.

INDEX

C

D

G

H

I

J

L

M

Q

R

S

T

U

V

W

Y